# The Last Days
# of the Renaissance

ALSO BY THEODORE K. RABB

*Renaissance Lives*

*Jacobean Gentleman*

*The Struggle for Stability in Early Modern Europe*

*The Thirty Years' War*

*Enterprise & Empire*

# The Last Days
# of the Renaissance

## *& the March to Modernity*

THEODORE K. RABB

BASIC
BOOKS

*A Member of the Perseus Books Group*
*New York*

Published by Basic Books,
A Member of the Perseus Books Group

Books published by Basic Books are available at special discounts
for bulk purchases in the United States by corporations,
institutions, and other organizations. For more information, please
contact the Special Markets Department at the Perseus Books
Group, 11 Cambridge Center, Cambridge MA 02142, or call
(617) 252-5298 or (800) 255-1514,
or e-mail special.markets@perseusbooks.com.

Library of Congress Cataloging-in-Publication Data
Rabb, Theodore K.
The last days of the Renaissance: & the march to modernity /
Theodore K. Rabb.
p. cm.
Includes bibliographical references and index.
ISBN-13: 978-0-465-06801-2 (alk. paper)
ISBN-10: 0-465-06801-4 (alk. paper)
1. Renaissance. I. Title.
CB369.R33 2006
940.2'1—dc22
2005030382
06 07 08 / 10 9 8 7 6 5 4 3 2 1

*For Alexandra, Juliet, Isabel, Emilia,
and Benjamin*

# Contents

# List of Illustrations

## Insert (between pages 118 and 119)

# *Acknowledgments*

My first debt is to Donald Fehr, who asked me to write this book for Basic Books, and to the editors who have succeeded him. My second is to Barbara Leavey, whose tireless supervision of details, especially the arrangement of the book's seventy illustrations, made the enterprise far less arduous than it would otherwise have been.

The book is the outcome of over forty-five years of teaching, and I cannot even begin to express my gratitude to the scores of students, both undergraduate and graduate, whose probings have helped bring its conclusions to the surface. The same is true of the many fellow-historians who have been willing to discuss its ideas with exemplary patience. They will recognize some of the argument in Chapter 4 from my 1974 *Struggle for Stability in Early Modern Europe*. In addition, I should note that I have on earlier occasions put forward quite explicitly the ideas and language in three sections of the book: The two parts of Chapter 6 emerge from a lecture delivered to the American Philosophical Society and then published in their *Transactions* in 1955, and from a talk I gave at Cambridge

University, under the kind hospitality of Sidney Sussex College in 1996; and the section on opera in Chapter 7 reproduces ideas first prepared for a conference on Opera and Society held at Princeton in 2004 and subsequently published in the *Journal of Interdisciplinary History* in 2005.

This book is at one level intended, not as a summary for my contemporaries, but as a template of European history for a new generation of historians. I therefore solicited the views of two younger colleagues on an earlier version. I am most grateful to both of them—Mordechai Feingold and Jacob Soll—for their care and their comments.

At another level the book is of course aimed at a general readership that does not often these days encounter large-scale narratives of the past. To gauge that response, I drafted my son Jonathan and my wife Tamar. To them my final debt is owed, and above all to Tamar, from whose questions and encouragement I have now been learning for almost fifty years.

# Introduction

When did the period that historians of the West call the Renaissance come to an end? To the general reader, this may seem to be a simple question; surely it was settled long ago. But in fact it has been largely ignored by scholars, who have spent far more time on the question of when the Renaissance began—a preoccupation fueled by those who deny that it was a distinct period at all, arguing instead that Dante for sure, Petrarch probably, and even the Medici and Martin Luther properly belong to the Middle Ages. For all the earnestness of such critiques, though, they have had minimal effect. In the textbooks and curricula through which history is taught, the Renaissance remains firmly enshrined. But the question "when did it end, and why?" opens up, as we shall see, a whole variety of ways of understanding European history.

More than a century ago, Jacob Burckhardt, the Swiss historian who founded the modern study of the period, had few doubts about periodization. Dealing exclusively with Italy, the crucible of the new outlook he called Renaissance civilization, he began his story in the fourteenth century and ended it in the sixteenth. Later expressions of the civilization outside Italy, such as the England of Thomas More or Shakespeare, were beyond his purview; he concentrated instead on the source and rise of the attitudes that were to capture all of Europe, and paid little attention to their dying away. That the Dutch historian Johan Huizinga was able to show, in response, that medieval attitudes persisted in northern Europe even while the Renaissance flourished in Italy merely confirmed that the complex question of origins is the one that historians like to pursue.

Indeed, it is not even clear what came next. In the story of art, where fine gradations of style and intent are more visible, the mutations that led to Mannerism and then the Baroque are unmistakable, and they can be linked to specific decades of the sixteenth century. In more general treatments, however, the labels for the succeeding period seem far less precise: Reformation? Counter-Reformation? Early Modern? Each has its advocates, and indeed I have used "Early Modern" in the title of a previous book. But none of these terms makes the task of defining a conclusion any easier. Even the most common of these progressions—the Renaissance followed by the Reformation (usually abbreviated as Ren/Ref)—is once again more useful in describing beginnings than endings. Few would claim, for instance, that the Renaissance was over by 1517, the conventional date for the beginning of the Reformation, or even by the 1540s, when the Counter-Reformation was well under way. After all, in the middle of the sixteenth century, the Escorial, perhaps the greatest monument of the Spanish Renaissance, had yet to be conceived, let alone built. The more all-encompassing label Early Modern, by contrast, sometimes includes the Renaissance, sometimes not, and in any event avoids the question of when "Early" became plain Modern. In general, endings always remain unclear, especially since those who study subsequent periods are no help. They have been equally preoccupied with beginnings, such as the roots of the Enlightenment or the Industrial Revolution, and rarely ask what died when their new world was born.

If the pages that follow take a different approach and focus on the last days of the Renaissance, it is because that reorientation may help us come up with a better understanding of the age it represents. By trying to determine what came to an end, and when, we may be able to illuminate some essential features of the Renaissance period and thus cast light on the qualities that set it apart from the periods that came before and after. The word "end" in this context is therefore relevant in *both* its meanings: the aims as well as the conclusion of the Renaissance. The argument will be, first, that a sea change overtook European civilization during the last half of the seventeenth century; and second, that these decades provide a vantage point from which we can understand the past as the Renaissance. What came next we will describe as the Age of Revolution, after which, at last, Modernity arrives.

Yet it must be emphasized that this is no Foucauldian enterprise, seeking to define the "episteme" of different ages. Against this danger the historian's instinctive blurring of edges, appreciation of inconsistency, and acceptance of contradiction is a necessary defense. Yet configurations do change; and, despite immense overlaps and irreconcilable ambiguities, fundamental shifts do take place. Unless we accept the border lines (loose, but visible nonetheless) that mark the progression from what Alistair Fowler has called one heterogeneity to the next, the attempt to understand the past will lose all focus.

This, therefore, is a book about periodization, a subject that historians often dismiss as a matter of personal preference, and therefore not worth serious inquiry. They may have to divide the past into separate eras when they describe undergraduate classes and academic vacancies, or when they grope for a book title; but the setting of boundaries is often regarded as a necessary evil, scarcely worthy of study in its own right. Medievalists who disagree with their neighbors about the end of antiquity or the beginning of the Renaissance, for instance, are engaged in the equivalent of a family squabble: The rights and wrongs are less important than the fruitfulness of the encounter.

Similarly, it is easy to dismiss the chronological metaphors to which writers of exam questions have to resort: the turning points, the watersheds, the milestones, and so forth. Although the explanation of change is at the heart of what historians do, we make it a virtue to soften our more far-reaching claims with reminders of continuity. Indeed, the taller the landmark, the stronger our insistence on the perspective that can make it disappear. Did the fall of Rome or the English Revolution really make much of a difference? There is a kind of modesty (or perhaps uneasiness) that stamps any attempt to distinguish among periods as quixotic at best and empty at worst. Moreover, one of the historian's duties is to be stern with the truth: No, Marie Antoinette did not say "Let them eat cake"; no, Columbus's contemporaries did not believe the earth was flat. But one wonders whether this austerity goes too far when there are no radical breaks with the past: not when Rome fell, not in 1789, not in Machiavelli's *Prince,* not in Luther's protest, never.

Despite the elusiveness of fundamental change, however, the subject of periodization has far-reaching implications, and its traditional dismissal evades the serious issues it raises. To enter this territory is to open up reams of counterexamples, not to mention the argument that the entire enterprise is doomed to failure. Is such an undertaking no more than an attempt to bring Hegel and the long-discredited notion of the "spirit of an age" back to life? The answer is that coherences (which, unlike "spirit," one can define in down-to-earth terms) are not mere figments of the imagination: It is not an imposition on fifteenth-century Florence, for instance, to suggest that the sports the citizens enjoyed reflected their social cleavages, their politics, and the topography of their city. The argument of this book is that the coherences that bind periods together are worth exposing, and that they are essential if one wishes to define and comprehend the shape of the past.

Moreover, there is no doubt that, in historical scholarship, debate is usually more productive than closure. My interpretations are unlikely to prompt universal agreement, let alone instant revisions of books and ideas or a definitive settlement of long-standing issues, but this is no cause for hesitation. The patterns into which the past is formed are too important, especially for those who have to try to convey its significance to the young, for us to take lightly the way we organize its bewildering variety. If what follows draws increased attention to the subject of periodization, that is all to the good.

There is much talk these days about historians' "constructing" rather than "discovering" the past. On that debate I take my lead from the philosopher R. G. Collingwood, who argued that what we call history is neither invented nor found: It is always the outcome of a constructive dialogue between the individual historian and the materials left to us by the past. He described the result as an understanding that was a better guide to human action than scientific method. If we took that admonition to heart and concentrated more on the substance that underlies the changes we explore, rather than the subjective criteria by which we portray the past, we might be able to fashion the broad, believable narratives that, although once at the heart of our enterprise, have recently given way to a focus on self-contained and often isolated issues or locales.

The task is made more urgent by the growing commitment to the teaching of world history, a subject where chronological dividing lines keep shifting with geography until one reaches the nineteenth century. To the extent that the history of the West is often the template on which global events are constructed—or at any rate taught, because in the classroom it is often the least unfamiliar and therefore the most useful organizing principle—one needs to be confident that the foundation has some substance. Here the notion that each observer "constructs" the subject anew, and that "facts" are an illusion, becomes most dangerous. Down that road lies the end of history as a basic means of educating a citizenry. If historians have an obligation to make sense of the past and to explain the origins of their world for the society in which they live, then the quest for coherence in their subject must be their primary goal.

Hence the book that follows, which seeks to identify a succession of fundamental shifts in historical periods from the Middle Ages to the present, with special attention to the time when the Renaissance dissolved into the Age of Revolution. Because that divide is the major pivot around which the argument turns, and indeed the reason for my title, I have offered a more thorough account of the process of change at this one juncture. It is in order to emphasize the centrality of the end of the Renaissance to my narrative that Chapter 6 proceeds at a level of detail not found elsewhere. Furthermore, to strengthen my case, I have not only suggested when, specifically, the Renaissance ended, but have extended the argument to two related, and no less thorny, issues of definition and periodization.

For there is no way to distinguish the Renaissance from the Age of Revolution that followed without indicating how they themselves differed, not just from one another but from what came before and after them as well. To speak of the Renaissance one has to indicate how it was distinct from the Middle Ages; and to describe the Age of Revolution, even if only briefly, one has to see how it contrasts with Modernity. As a result, although our principal concern is the transformation from Renaissance to Revolution, that very investigation implies judgments about the transformations that created the former and undermined the latter. A book that asks what changed in the second half of the seventeenth century therefore has to suggest (albeit in outline) how we might look at the two other great shifts that have shaken western culture since medieval times. Consequently, the periodization I propose addresses four distinct and coherent patterns that have ruled the West in succession: during the Middle Ages, the Renaissance, the Age of Revolution, and (still in formation) Modernity. By seeing how these patterns crystallized and then dissolved (with particular attention to the second), we will move, in four large steps, from the time of Charlemagne to the present.

*Princeton, New Jersey*
*October 2005*

# The Last Days
# of the Renaissance

✎

*Chapter One*

# THE UNITIES OF
# THE MEDIEVAL WEST

*T*he people of the Renaissance injected into European history a yearning for an ideal long dead: the political order and the cultural coherence of ancient Rome. To make that dream come true, they had to break free from some of the structures and beliefs that eventually replaced the Roman Empire after its collapse in the early fifth century. It had taken more than half a millennium for that new unity to emerge in the West. Around the year 800, Charlemagne had attempted to claim the mantle of the emperors, and he had put a distinctive political and cultural stamp on his age; but his ascendancy was a brief interlude within a long period of fragmentation and disruption. Indeed, the very absence of the documentation that might allow us to form a fuller picture of these centuries is an indication of the centrifugal forces that were at work.

It may seem like hubris for historians to use the lack of materials to call this era the Dark Ages, but the rarity of written records from these centuries does signify the weakness of the governmental institutions and the intellectual life that are the main creators of such records. Although remarkable works of art and literature have survived (one has but to think of the *Book of Kells*), many of the building blocks that permit us to reconstruct a past civilization have disappeared. We cannot securely approximate population size or the contours of daily life; we know nothing about the rulers of most areas; and we consider ourselves fortunate when a rare source such as Bede or Einhard allows us to put a little flesh on the bare bones of obscure events. That there seem to be almost no connections among the few stories we can tell—the struggles of the papacy, the expanding settlement of the Venetian lagoon, the Christian counteroffensive in Spain, the changing relations with the Eastern Church, the wars that engaged Franks or Saxons, the voyages of the Irish missionaries and the Vikings—merely emphasizes the fragmentation of this half-millennium.

During the 350 years that followed, however, from the late tenth through the early fourteenth centuries, there can be no mistaking the community of institutions and ideas that arose and gave shape to the period that has come to be seen as the flowering of the Middle Ages. The bonds that held this civilization together—shifting and developing, to be sure, but recognizable nonetheless—can here be summarized only briefly, but they have to be outlined because they formed the edifice against which successive generations revolted. As they did so, these generations were to bring about the reorderings and the new coherence we call the Renaissance.

∽

The institutions that united medieval Europe may have varied in appearance and impact by country and period, but they shared a fundamental structure and purpose that is inescapable. Among these features, which between them created basic uniformities in the life of the continent's peoples, were the Church, warfare, servitude, urban structures, and the intersection of politics, law, and society.

No organization could match the Church as the rock on which the coherence of western European civilization was built during the Middle Ages. Not only was its presence felt in every village, but it was indeed organized. The Church's hierarchy was clear-cut and, for all its adaptations to local customs, saints, and practices, its representatives knew exactly where they stood in relation to one another, and they formed a single connected network that spanned the continent. In this regard, the Church was the true successor to the Roman Empire.

Although in earlier centuries the authority of popes had often been uncertain, by the end of the eleventh century, thanks to the drama at Canossa in 1077 and the launching of the first Crusade by Urban II in 1095 (followed by the capture of Jerusalem four years later), no doubts could have remained. At Canossa an emperor had knelt in the snow to demonstrate his submission to a pope, and 150 years later princes and kings were still conceding victory to Rome in a series of struggles over Church appointments. To many, the successes of Innocent III in this investiture controversy during the early thirteenth century must have given papal authority an aura of invincibility. Even though the papacy was to find its struggles with secular rulers increasingly difficult during the centuries to come, it long remained, as an institution, a powerful force binding Europe together, from Trondheim to Taormina, from Lisbon to Lübeck.

At the local level, thousands of priests, friars, and monks reinforced this unity, despite their oft-remarked inadequacies as spiritual guardians and exemplars for their contemporaries. Their very pervasiveness as representatives of the Church helped shape a unity that overcame even the widest disparities. Their status within secular society was always the same, as was their subordination to clearly identified superiors and their role within the larger structure of which they were a part. Whatever assistance was available for the poor and sick came from them; and for everyone they represented literacy, counsel, and the only universally accepted moral guidance and access to the supernatural that was available to the society. However far a traveler might have journeyed, he could be sure that at each new destination the clerics would be a familiar sight, transcending all boundaries and divides.

Alongside the universality of the buildings and people that constituted the physical presence of the Church was its role in day-to-day existence. Here the liturgy, the ceremonies, and the festivals that comprised its public occasions, and the consultations and rites of passage that brought it into its parishioners' private worlds, made it a constant and unavoidable accompaniment to the lives of all people, whether great or humble. The Church was the most fundamental of all the influences that shaped the cohesion of medieval Europe.

A second unifying institution was the practice of war. Europe's small, isolated, and self-sufficient communities had been vulnerable to marauders and passing conquerors for centuries, from the first tribal incursions into the Roman Empire until the Vikings. In response, these communities had fashioned a unique system of self-defense. Instead of developing the centrally organized forces that had been typical of ancient regimes such as Assyria, Sparta, or Rome, and more recently of the tribes that had poured in from the East, the Europeans worked from below, assembling whatever capacity they had for warfare in the locality.

Living in a politically and economically fragmented world, they were hardly capable of consolidating far-flung manpower into a unified military effort. Instead, they relied on the most potent figure in the area to put together a fighting force. This was, quite naturally, the principal landowner, the lord, who was probably the only person who could afford the horse, armor, and weaponry that were the essential equipment for leadership on the battlefield (fig. 1). In return for his protection, and for being allowed to take some of the produce of his land, the people of the area not only worked the land but also joined whatever small armed band he put together at a time of danger or war.

The significance of this familiar pattern, described in every textbook on the Middle Ages, is that, with minor variations, it was common to every region. The system of recruitment thus shaped the similarity of social and political as well as military conditions that prevailed throughout Europe. And just as each villager had to observe his rights and obligations with respect to his lord, so, too, did the lords themselves maintain intricate and sometimes overlapping linkages with one another. For all the complexities, however, this set of arrangements did serve its central purposes, warfare and defense, quite well. It was even capable of gathering together sizeable armies, as the launching of the Crusades demonstrated.

Basic tactics and strategies, as in every age, were universal, and indeed had changed little since antiquity. The invention of the stirrup had given cavalry a newly dominant role (which justified the importance of the knight on horseback), and the bow was growing in importance. But, in essence, combat was the

*Fig. 1 When the* Bayeux Tapestry *shows the Normans landing in England, it not only emphasizes the importance of the horse to the medieval warrior but reminds us, in the design of the boats, that the Normans were Vikings.*

same throughout Europe, usually dependent on the valor and the skills of the man on the horse as he clashed with his counterparts on the opposing side (fig. 2). Hence the equation of the noble and the warrior; hence the need for the trappings of chivalry to give higher meaning to the sheer brutality of war; and hence the jousts and tournaments, the crucial training grounds for the knight's techniques. By the tenth century, the image and the practice of nobility, rooted in war, was universally accepted. In the secular realm, as in the spiritual, a single institution and model of behavior embodied authority in every region.

*Fig. 2    The centrality of the mounted knight in medieval warfare is demon-strated by this scene from the* Bayeux Tapestry *of the 1070s.*

If we move, next, from Europe's military practices to its economic and social structure, we take but a small step. Decades of research have revealed the inconsistencies and in-adequacies of describing this symbiosis as "feudalism." Rather than enter that minefield, therefore, it might make sense to view the relations between those who worked the land and those who owned it as a system of servitude. For servitude was the common experience that united agricultural laborers (and many townsmen, too) throughout the continent. A tiny minor-ity owned what Marx called the means of production, and a vast majority served the minority's needs. To be more precise, a peasantry tilled lands it did not own, and in return received protection and a basic subsistence. The cat's cradle of rights and obligations that has been called feudalism revolved around this economic and social relationship, and it is a rather arid question of priorities to ask whether military prowess led to wealth and status or vice versa. Either way, the dependence of the many on the few was the same.

In some areas the servitude included a prohibition against movement, which was the heart of serfdom. Even in regions without serfs, however, the basic experiences of the vast majority of Europe's population were so similar in the duties and privileges they could expect that a villager from Denmark would quickly have understood the conditions that dominated the life of his counterpart in Calabria. Proportions are impossible to calculate, but the tiny percentage of the population made up of property owners did not vary greatly by area—nor was it that different in the rest of the world. Nevertheless, the superstructure of oaths of fealty and homage, of distinct feudal rights, and of accepted connections between lord and peasant not only distinguished the economic and social structure of the West's agrarian areas (that is, the preponderance of settled lands) from those of rural regions outside Europe but also gave its people a community of custom, behavior, and identity that bound them together.

The exception in this web of relations was the town, usually a settlement of more than 1,000 people defended by walls or water, and its larger sibling, the city (usually at least 4,000–5,000 strong). Before the eleventh century, cities were a negligible presence on the European scene. By the end of the thirteenth century, thanks to a long period of rising population, booming trade, and proliferating markets, they were widely familiar, especially in northern Italy, the Low Countries, and the

Rhineland. In some of these cities the numbers had climbed to between 50,000 and 100,000—most notably in Italy, which had seven such centers, stretching from Palermo to Venice; the north, by contrast, might have had only London, Ghent, Bruges, and Cologne. The largest city of them all, Paris, probably reached a population of 200,000 by the late thirteenth century. These dozen cities, housing about 1.5 million people between them, most likely contained about half the city dwellers of Europe; yet they, in turn, comprised no more than a small fraction (probably less than 10 percent) of a Europe that was overwhelmingly rural.

Nevertheless, the relative scarcity of urban residents should not mask their importance as yet another indicator of the regularities that bound this society together. Although as a group they were exceptional in medieval Europe—not only because they remained a tiny minority but also because they often enjoyed more economic and political rights than their rural neighbors—they themselves had a great deal in common. Even if their inhabitants traveled to distant cities, as did the Italians and the Netherlanders, who moved back and forth between their two regions, and the Hanseatic merchants, who criss-crossed the northern seas, they would have found much that was familiar.

The physical setting, for instance, would have been largely recognizable, regardless of different architectural styles and the necessities imposed by varying climates. Most towns and cities were built around a castle, a major church, or an imposing municipal building. In front of this edifice would have been a rare open space of some size, the site used for markets and public ceremonies. With the town hemmed in by walls or water, there would have been room for wide roads suitable for carts only between the principal gates. Elsewhere, warrens of narrow lanes and alleys would have interlaced neighborhoods of tightly packed houses, usually of three or four stories, clustered around wells, open sewers, street-level shops, taverns, workshops, and the occasional public building, patrician residence, or religious establishment.

Social and economic organization would have been familiar, too. Craft guilds were becoming essential features in cities throughout Europe, and their privileges and regulations—legal rights, requirements of apprenticeship, standards of production, provisions for the welfare of members—would have been instantly recognizable, despite local variants. Although the goods that artisans manufactured did not yet challenge the preeminence of agriculture in Europe's economy, in all areas there had arisen a kaleidoscope of occupations and products, many of recent origin, and noticeable disparities of wealth.

Below the artisans in the social order were the day laborers; here, as in the countryside, they were relegated to the bottom rung of the social order. Their lives would have seemed familiar well beyond the borders of Europe, but those for whom they worked—the traders and merchants who stood at the top of urban society—were, by the thirteenth century, making an essential contribution to the unity and coherence of Europe. Communication and travel may have been slow—it took twelve days, at top speed, to get a message from Marseilles to Paris, and more than two months for a traveler, going at a steady pace, to reach Rome from Rouen—but Europe's roads, as well as its more easily traversed rivers and seas, were thronged not only with pilgrims, messengers, migrants, and soldiers, but also with the salesmen who were shaping a continent-wide economy as they traded their goods. Commercial practices, financial instruments, and the solution of such technical problems as monetary exchange in an era of proliferating currencies were marked by a uniformity that bound Scandinavia to Spain, Italy to Ireland. Moreover, the major focal points of international trade, the cities of northern Italy and the Netherlands, the Hanseatic League, and the fairs of Champagne, ensured that commodities such as cloth and silk moved smoothly across great distances. The leading figures in this world might gain the ear of kings; but usually, along with their counterparts in local commerce, they focused their political ambitions on the city governments they dominated. Yet their connections and shared interests created a community that, almost by definition, transcended linguistic boundaries and imposed an essential armature of economic behavior on all of Europe.

The consequences of these institutional, social, and economic arrangements were visible in another arena, the political forms one encounters throughout Europe. Although the pyramidal hierarchic model was always taken for granted—that is, one or a few at the top of the social order, enjoying a God-given right to rule, and then increasing numbers at each level of descent down to the mass of the people at the bottom—it had its quirks and oddities in different regions. Social deference and homage gave to aristocracies and princes everywhere the right to make decisions about taxes, war, and the other major issues that communities faced. But localities throughout Europe also observed, during the Middle Ages, crucial rights of representation and consultation that gave Europe its unique political and legal character.

This representation started at the village level, where there is evidence that councils of elders decided local matters throughout medieval times. In towns, those functions were undertaken by guilds, which became the basic form of urban organization and the foundation on which town councils, mayors, and city governments were built. In the countryside, too, squires and lords expected to be consulted when princes and kings had demands to make. Everywhere, various types of assembly, whether known as estates, diets, or parliaments, began to gather together the representatives of a region so that they could advise rulers about conditions in their territories and help carry out policies such as the raising of taxes.

Essential to the operation of this system were two of the distinctive and unifying features of medieval life: the oath and the contract. When homage or fealty was offered, it was sworn. The lord and those who served him took it for granted that their relationship had to be sanctified by the religious power of the oath. What was thus brought into being was a set of social obligations and responsibilities that, whether written down or not, took the form of a contract. The resultant assumption that mutual rights and duties bound everyone together was not only omnipresent but also one of the period's chief legacies to future ages.

At the highest level of society, princes, following the example of Charlemagne, preferred religious to contractual sanction for their authority. At coronation ceremonies throughout Europe, new monarchs were anointed with holy oil, and gradually the theory arose that kings ruled by divine right. They might have an earthly body, but they also had a presence ordained by heaven; this gave them such magical attributes as the "king's touch," the belief that a royal hand, if laid on a sufferer, could cure scrofula. Solemn rituals and ceremonies confirmed these powers, for public celebrations were as important in secular as in religious affairs.

Law, in turn, derived its compelling force both from the public occasions at which it was administered and from the monarch's authority. It might operate through a codification derived from Roman law, as in most of the Continent, or through statute and precedent, as in England, but the principle of *Rex est Lex* was fundamental to almost every legal system. And everywhere the Church, as a distinct estate, would have had its own presence in representative assemblies and an independent hierarchy of courts. By and large, therefore, the communal, regional, and princely structures under whose political and legal control the western Europeans lived would have seemed familiar, no matter how far one of its inhabitants might have traveled from home ground.

∞

In cultural life, a similar homogeneity was achieved. The principal unifying force was again the Church because it was the home of all education and the chief moral and intellectual authority of the time. The ways the Church shaped the outlook and beliefs of its flock were manifold, however, and one cannot always describe the major attributes of medieval culture as mere manifestations of its teachings. Certainly the Church contributed vital elements to the cultural unity of the West by helping to shape coherences of thought and art that were the equivalents of the links that pervaded Europe's institutional and material life. Yet the primacy of religion does not mean that everything people wrote, painted, sculpted, and built served only spiritual ends.

It is worth recalling, for instance, the weaknesses that tempered the victory of the Christian faith, not only in many sectors of an illiterate and often semi-pagan population but also throughout the northern and eastern fringes of the continent, where missionaries were still active during the twelfth century. Similarly, although Europe's educational system was run overwhelmingly by and for the clergy, this did not preclude a growing admiration for ancient pagans such as Virgil and Aristotle. Religious instruction was no monolith, as is evident, too, in the acceptance and indeed encouragement of local cults and practices. Thus we need an important qualification—that religion's influence did not always promote standardization—when we acknowledge the Church's role as the foundation for medieval Europe's creative life. What is unmistakable, though, is that it helped form the ideas of the elite by sponsoring a learned culture that was truly international; at the same time, it shaped grass roots assumptions through such phenomena as the rapid spread of the belief in purgatory or the almost universal recognition that a halo in a work of art was the mark of a holy figure. If we identify other sources of cultural coherence in medieval Europe, we do so only in the context of the Church's all-embracing presence.

Most notable among these sources was the emergence of a system of education that promoted common goals and standards. The basic curriculum consisted of the seven liberal arts: the Trivium of grammar, logic, and rhetoric for the bachelor's degree; and the Quadrivium of arithmetic, geometry, music, and astronomy for the master's. When, in the thirteenth century, a further level was added, consisting of three philosophies (natural, moral, and metaphysical), the system was complete, and it became available in this form at universities from Uppsala to Salamanca. Moreover, the language that the literate shared, Latin, strengthened the bonds among the educated throughout the continent. Vernaculars may have been developing, and the epic poems that are among the glories of medieval Europe, from *Beowulf* to the *Divine Comedy,* were a foretaste of divisions within its culture. Yet homogeneity was still the norm, as is apparent from even the briefest glance at the cathedrals that still dominate so much of the landscape, whether the Romanesque of Brescia and Ely or the Gothic of Cologne and Chartres.

Social and political ideas, theology, literature, and the arts merely emphasized the breadth of this uniformity. Here, however, we can mention only a few of the many themes and assumptions that characterized the culture of these centuries.

One of the most revealing was its choice of heroes, which focused primarily on biblical figures and the saints of the Christian tradition. There were shifts, to be sure. The cult of the Virgin, for example, was a late arrival on the scene. But the martyrs and the holy men and women who dominated artistic representations were revered in all areas, even when localities added their own special heroes. These were the models of virtue whom everyone could venerate.

Secular heroes may have been less admirable, but they too won status under the aura of religion. Crusaders, above all, committed as they were to defeating the deniers of Christ's divinity, offered this society a potent ideal. That Charlemagne was the subject of a stained-glass window in the cathedral at Chartres (see rear cover) was a reflection not of his far-flung military prowess but of his undertaking one particular expedition: an incursion into Spain that began the reconquest of that peninsula from its Muslim rulers. Because a crusading spirit was the source of the emperor's fame, Charlemagne's assault on fellow Christians in Spain was ignored; their ambush of the emperor's rear guard as the army returned to

France was transformed into a cowardly assault by infidels. And this legend, in turn, created a bevy of doomed heroes who were celebrated in the *Song of Roland* because they died for the glory of God. That the Crusades had a darker side—their initiation of the European tradition of persecution of the Jews, their viciousness toward other Christians when turned against Constantinople or the Albigensians, their brutalities amidst the often more sophisticated Muslims—was of no consequence amidst the honors accorded to those who fought in the name of God.

The elevation of valor in battle above all other qualities in the definition and self-image of Europe's nobility was a heritage from classical times. The ideal was shared by every leader and lord, whether the ruler of an Italian hilltop town or a Viking marauder, and it was reinforced by the importance in battle of the mounted warrior—the preserve of the rich and powerful. To sheer prowess, however, there was added in the late Middle Ages the chivalric ideal. This concept of the knight as a self-effacing man who fought in God's name, served his lady, and was connected to the softer realms of poetry and music gave a gentler edge to knightly heroism. When described by the troubador or set amidst the trappings of courtly love, the idealism of the knight became essential to his image. And it had its visible manifestation during the celebrations of skill and decorum that constituted the tournament and the joust—each a growing presence amongst the rituals and ceremonies of medieval life. These might not have been frequent in all areas, nor was the chivalric ideal as honored in practice as it was in literature and the arts, but there is no escaping the vision of the knightly hero, in his various manifestations, as a unifying image in European culture.

In all definitions of heroism, however, sanctity was the overarching value. Thus, Louis IX of France and Thomas à Becket of England, like Charlemagne, might have been skilled at politics and administration, but they were revered only because of their reputation for piety. For them, the reverence led to sainthood. But even less spectacular manifestations of devoutness than Louis's leadership during a Crusade to the East, or Becket's martyrdom in Canterbury Cathedral, inspired the greatest respect. For many centuries the monk, dedicated solely to prayer and good works, was the exemplary figure in society. Not only did his prayers serve the entire community, but it was he who led the continuing missionary effort to bring Christianity to all regions of Europe. When monastic standards declined, the preaching friars, notably the orders founded by St. Francis and St. Dominic in the early thirteenth century, took their place as the embodiments of self-denying holiness. When St. Francis joined a Crusade and, in a famous moment, crossed battle lines in Egypt so that he could bring the word of God to the Muslim commander, he embodied the combined ideal of holiness and heroism.

Essential to the model of virtue offered by monks, nuns, and friars was their poverty. They may have observed their vows only fitfully, but the very attempt to emulate Jesus' disdain for worldly goods excited admiration. The concomitant distrust of material success was, at least in theory, another widespread feature of medieval society.

All these attitudes were united by the belief that Europe's social hierarchy, like the authority of its rulers, was divinely ordained. A great chain of being assigned appropriate roles to everyone on Earth, linking them even to the kings whose authority came directly from God. Social and political values, in other words, were yet another element in the cohesiveness of medieval Europe.

～

Helping to create and justify these ideals was a set of basic assumptions that dominated intellectual and artistic life. Foremost, as will have become apparent, was the determination to bring religious beliefs to bear on every aspect of existence. The supernatural gave shape and meaning to all human affairs. For scholars and theologians, the task was to explain how that influence operated and how it was to be understood: an effort that required an array of techniques ranging from the study of canon law to the interpretation of holy texts.

One particularly powerful instrument can be singled out, though, not only because it was to have such a fruitful life long after the Middle Ages but also because it was an idea associated with the most influential theologian of the early Church, St. Augustine. This instrument was the resort to allegory as a vital means of uncovering truth. Allegory also became a basic window into the meaning of works of art; it often seems that no medieval artifact, whether the shape of a cathedral or the depiction of a person, was unaffected by allegorical purpose. Most cathedrals, for instance, were formed into the shape of a cross—or, more elaborately, as an outline of Mary cradling the infant Jesus (fig. 3). Similarly, depictions of holy scenes showed little interest in perspective or other techniques of representing physical reality, but instead focused on symbolic concerns, such as the way the size of a figure might indicate its relative spiritual importance or an attribute such as a lion or a book might define a specific person or message (fig. 4).

A good example is the attitude toward light. It was believed that God's influence entered the world along rays of light, that

*Fig. 3 When seen from the air, Peterborough Cathedral, built mainly in the twelfth and early thirteenth centuries, reveals how effectively Christian symbols, in this example the cross, shaped medieval art and architecture.*

these streams were the channels of grace; the obsession with the illumination of Gothic cathedrals, therefore, was not merely a practical concern but an attempt to expand the presence of the divine in a sacred space. The same motive lay behind the enthusiasm for optics, the most effective branch of medieval natural science. One might even argue that the invention of eyeglasses, probably in the thirteenth century, was a silent tribute to the power of allegory.

Many other distinguishing features define medieval intellectual life, but especially salient were those, like the fascination with allegory, that supported a central enterprise: explaining

*Fig. 4 This twelfth-century manuscript illumination shows the power of allegory and symbol in medieval art. The subject, at the bottom, is the Marriage of the Virgin to St. Joseph. Above, surrounding Christ, his fingers raised in blessing and the open book showing his Word, are the four Evangelists whose Gospels reveal his Word: St. Matthew the tax collector holds a box for collecting taxes; the eagle is the attribute of St. John; and the winged ox and lion are the attributes, respectively, of St. Luke and St. Mark. The last three all hold the books that contain their Gospels.*

and disseminating the teachings of the Bible and the early Christian Fathers. What this entailed was, first, a dedication to traditional knowledge and an admiration for those who produced illuminating commentary on the past. If this occasionally led to a fascination with pagan antiquity (most notably an attachment to Virgil that led some to claim him as a prophet of Christianity), such feelings were inevitably tinged with unease (fig. 5). Only the recovery of Aristotle, largely through contacts with Muslim scholarship, seemed without blemish, particularly when Aristotelian rationality was blended almost seamlessly into theological discourse by its most eminent late-medieval exponent, Thomas Aquinas. The works of Aquinas also reflected

*Fig. 5    That the early sixteenth-century Dutch artist Lucas van Leyden twice engraved the legend of Virgil's being left dangling in a basket halfway up a wall when he tried to visit the daughter of the Emperor Augustus suggests how popular the memory of the Roman poet remained in medieval Europe.*

(and exemplified) the preference for the methods of dialectic logic in intellectual inquiry. This system of statement, counterstatement, and response had its counterpart in the disputation, the juxtaposition of opposing arguments that was the main mechanism (alongside the lecture) of medieval university instruction. All these endeavors were justified by their spiritual purpose: Learning for its own sake was unacceptable. Nevertheless, the scholarly achievements of the age, starting in its monasteries and expanding into its universities, were one of its glories.

This outline of some of the landmarks of medieval culture cannot do justice to its artistic and philosophic achievements, let alone its educational innovations, its political and social norms, or its spiritual ideals. But the focus on the major unities that held a civilization together means that much has to be neglected. And it means, also, that one must leave aside the exceptional and the rare, such as the medieval flowering of mysticism, which—although a notable expression of religiosity—did not form overarching linkages across the disparate regions and localities of western Europe.

⚈⚈

This brief sketch, therefore, is not intended as a portrait of medieval society or culture; it serves (as will similar overviews in the following chapters) as a means of emphasizing the broad reach of the central features of an age. Nor is it intended as an argument for uniformity or universality; there were exceptions, incongruities, and contradictions aplenty. But there was sufficient common ground within this heterogeneity to leave no doubt that Europe during these centuries deserves to be seen as a distinct civilization that enjoyed shared values and patterns of behavior.

Moreover, the features that have been outlined here are presented primarily as background to the fundamental change that overtook Europe in the fourteenth and fifteenth centuries. This was to be a time when some of the most cherished assumptions, institutions, and activities of the Middle Ages came under fierce attack—a series of assaults that dissolved the sense of coherence that medieval society had created. Although much of the medieval world was to survive, a different heterogeneity was gradually to crystallize during the next three hundred years. It is to that next period in Europe's history, the age of the Renaissance—and in particular the way it, too, came to an end—that we must now turn.

# Chapter Two

# EUROPE RESHAPED:
# TOWARD THE RENAISSANCE

*T*he assault on the values of the Middle Ages that first made its mark in the fourteenth century involved Church and laity, practice and belief, institutions and ideas: a spectrum of discontent that relentlessly eroded the cohesion I have just outlined.

The erosion of papal authority was the most dramatic sign of dissatisfaction with the received wisdom of the high Middle Ages, and in some respects it was the most astonishing. In the first half of the thirteenth century, the pope's triumphs in the investiture controversy had seemed unequivocally to confirm his claims to supremacy over secular rulers. Less than a hundred years later those claims were in ruins.

Particularly disastrous was the reign of Boniface VIII (1295–1303), an interventionist whose demands were rejected by kings throughout Europe, from Aragon to Denmark. His attempts to assert his power, notably in two papal bulls that first forbade secular rulers from taxing the clergy and then proclaimed the superiority of popes over kings, merely backfired. Eventually, the most powerful of his rivals, Philip IV of France, took drastic steps to end the interference, and in 1303 he ordered his troops to imprison Boniface for a few days. A further indignity arrived in 1309, when Boniface's successor, Clement V, moved the papal seat from Rome to the French-speaking city of Avignon, on the border of France. Ideas followed action as theorists drew sharper lines between the authority of the papacy and the power of princes. One of them, Marsiglio of Padua, who was employed at the French court, went so far as to make an unequivocal case for the superior authority of the state. Christ's behavior, he noted in his *Defensor Pacis* (1324), was the decisive example:

> It plainly appears that He permitted Himself to be taken and led to the court of Pilate, vicar of the Roman emperor, and endured that He be condemned and handed over by the same judge to the extreme punishment.

The widespread and effective aggressiveness of secular rulers, particularly toward the Church, was to be a dominant feature of Renaissance Europe.

Nor was the "Babylonian Captivity" in Avignon the end of papal traumas. Although the Avignon period lasted less than seventy years, it was followed by four decades of Schism, a period when the jostling by rival political forces for control of the papacy produced two (and, for a while, three) competing claimants to the see of St. Peter. Only by summoning a general Council of the Church—in itself a threat to the sovereignty of the pope—were the West's ecclesiastical leaders able to restore unity. Not until the mid-1400s was Rome again able to reassert its sway over the institution it ruled. By then it was unmistakable that the papacy had lost its ability to challenge the monarchs it had once cowed. A new era had been born.

To some degree related, but arising from much broader concerns, were signs of growing dissatisfaction with religious doctrine and practice. The medieval Church had been able to encompass a vast spectrum of belief. From the maze of details beloved by canon lawyers to the stark mysticism of Joachim of Fiore in the twelfth century or St. Bonaventure in the thirteenth; from the complex rituals of well-organized monks to the simple rites conducted by virtually illiterate parish priests; and from the elaborate sermons in richly ornate cathedrals to the preaching of poverty by Franciscans in the streets: All were accepted as paths to salvation and all redounded to the greater glory of God. But in the late 1300s, buffeted by crisis, the Church seemed to lose its ability to embrace those who sought new paths to their faith.

Where once Rome had been able to absorb the ideas of a dissenter such as St. Francis when he called for simpler forms of devotion, its response now was different. Around 1400, two potent demands for a simpler doctrine and ritual arose—one in England, the other in Bohemia—but this time the reaction was a turn to persecution and violence. Indicative of the papacy's new weakness was its helplessness when some English courtiers successfully defended from the Church hierarchy a combative theologian, John Wycliffe, who started to criticize traditional practices in the 1370s. Wycliffe's doubts about ecclesiastical finances, formal ceremonies, and clerical behavior, and his demand for greater reliance on the Bible, were regarded as a dangerous "barking against the Church," but there was nothing the authorities could do to stop him. Not until his death in 1384 did opinion begin to shift. Eventually, Wycliffe's bones were exhumed and thrown into a river, and his followers, the Lollards, were driven underground. But by then the damage had been done: A rift in beliefs had opened, and it was only to widen during the next century.

More serious still was the critique by a Bohemian cleric and professor who had been influenced by Wycliffe, Jan Hus. His demand for a religion centered on biblical precept, individual faith, and a more egalitarian ritual came to be identified with his insistence that, in the mass, the congregation should share the wine as well as the bread. This "communion in both kinds" was seen as a serious symbolic threat to the distinct superiority of the priest, and hence to the Church itself. In earlier centuries a way might have been found to accommodate such divergent views, but now the response was unyielding. Hus left the political protection he enjoyed in Bohemia to make his case before a general Church Council that was embroiled in the fights over the Schism, and, safe-conduct notwithstanding, he was executed in 1415.

Again, however, it was too late to put the genie definitively back into the bottle. Hus's followers assembled an army and fought to keep his ideas alive; they forced acceptance of communion in both kinds for themselves, and eventually (like the Lollards) they provided a seedbed for the movement that was to destroy the unity of western Christendom in the following century. As in the case of papal authority, an essential component of the unity of medieval society had been tested and found wanting.

⮑⮒

No less potent challenges to medieval assumptions and prac-tices arose in the secular realm. Here, though, the impetus came not so much from disillusionment as from the pressure of external forces, including technology and disease. A notewor-thy example was the conduct of war. The last decisive battle fought by the methods that had served Europe for centuries was probably Agincourt in 1415. Although tactically the out-come was a stunning surprise—humble English infantry and archers defeating the cream of French cavalry—in equipment, training, and recruitment the armies would have seemed rela-tively familiar to their ancestors of the twelfth century. And yet, during the next century, as in the stature of the papacy and in religion, a fundamental divide was to be passed.

The upheaval in military affairs, however, had a much sim-pler origin: a technological breakthrough, the use of gunpow-der. Uncertainty may surround its earliest appearance in the West, but there is no doubt that the use of explosives in war gathered momentum in the 1400s. By the end of the century, the fortification that had stood at the heart of medieval de-fenses, the castle, had lost its traditional impregnability because its walls were now vulnerable to the new weaponry. The conse-quences were to affect not only strategic planning and the eco-nomics of war but also such different worlds as the architecture of the country house and the design of cities. Larger armies, expanded forms of siegecraft, more elaborate systems of ranks, and training in new skills all transformed the life of the soldier and the tasks of those who organized troops and kept them in the field. At the same time, gunpowder, with its capacity to kill indiscriminately from a distance, had a profound impact on knightly valor and its link with social distinction. Why should the noble have to be a warrior if individual bravery no longer determined success on the battlefield?

Questions like this, which reshaped attitudes toward authority, and even some of the definitions of social and political hierarchy, might have begun with the technology of armaments, but eventually they fed a broad torrent of change. In more than minor respects, one could define the Renaissance as the age that came to terms with the invention of gunpowder.

⮦⮧

The most shattering of the blows to medieval society in the fourteenth century was the Black Death, a series of devastations that began in the 1340s. As with gunpowder, this was an external force at work, but its consequences seemed limitless. Some historians have argued that the rising population of the high Middle Ages was already straining at the limits of Europe's resources by 1300; yet there can be no doubt that the sharp reversal of centuries of expansion was primarily the result of outbreaks of famine in the early fourteenth century and then, far more destructively, of plague. However they are construed, the numbers are astounding. Even a conservative estimate would suggest that, by 1450, Europe contained at most one half, and possibly little more than one third, of the number of people who had lived there 150 years earlier. Despite a few areas that avoided the worst of the disasters, the grim legacy of loss on this scale was felt throughout the continent.

Not all the effects of declining population were adverse. Economic and social winners flourished alongside the losers: Wage-earners did well even as food sellers fared poorly. In terms of the break with the medieval past, though, the demographic cataclysm of the 1400s was one of the surest signs that an old order had been destroyed. During the next two centuries, not only did industry and commerce have to develop in new directions but so too did structures of employment, and thus the relations among social classes.

Where political relationships were concerned, changes in traditional assumptions became inevitable in the wake of the erosion of Church authority, the reorientation of warfare, and the effects of plague and economic depression. In the struggles with the papacy, kings had made claims of independent authority in the 1300s; and though they did not follow up on these claims for some time, they gave notice that they had their own justifications, rooted in divine right, secular law, precedent, and their relations with the people they ruled, for making demands on their subjects that no superior could overturn. That more aggressive stance was only strengthened by the new conditions that governed military affairs.

The feature of gunpowder that had the most far-reaching consequences, outside the battlefield, was its cost. The substance itself was fairly cheap to produce, but the new weapons and skills it required, and the defensive structures it demanded, made its application prohibitively expensive. Casting cannon and cannon balls, manufacturing hand guns and their ammunition, training soldiers in the use of these devices, and building bastions to protect city walls: All depended on financial outlays without precedent in the Middle Ages. This shift was exacerbated by the slow dissolution of the system by which medieval militias had been recruited. Increasingly, the traditional feudal levy, consisting of able-bodied men who fought with the overlord to fulfill their obligations as tenants, had been replaced by mercenaries. This "bastard" feudalism, which substituted cash for service, was yet another signpost toward a very different future. By the late 1400s, therefore, it was clear that only princes of considerable means had the resources for the new kind of war, and that the once-redoubtable noble in his castle was helpless to resist them. The inevitable results were not long in coming: Those who could afford to equip an army began to assume new powers over their subjects, notably by imposing ever higher taxes (largely, of course, to help pay for these very guns and troops).

Demographic, economic, and social changes helped this process along. Of the many effects of the Black Death, the most revolutionary was its impact on labor, wages, and servitude. With a much smaller population to draw on, landowners, whose fields had to be tilled, animals tended, and harvests raised, were forced to find new ways to attract the manpower they needed. There was no point in insisting on feudal obligations or traditional forms of servitude if the people were unavailable. The alternative, offering wages to free laborers, not only liberated hundreds of thousands who previously had been tied to the land but also set in motion a major shift in social relations.

The freeing of western Europe's serfs was the essential prerequisite for the growth of cities and the small but important improvements in opportunities for advancement that were to benefit succeeding generations. Both developments, together with the replacement of servitude by wage labor, caused difficulties for the landed aristocracy, and in the major trading centers of northern Italy and the Netherlands their already weakened position was soon to dwindle to virtual insignificance. Even in areas that the leading landowners had traditionally controlled, the new pressures from below left them ever more vulnerable to the demands of princes from above. The struggle was to be long and hard, but by the late 1400s the balance of power within kingdoms and principalities was shifting toward the ruler at the center. The structure of politics would soon be transformed beyond recall as princes and monarchs gradually imposed new demands and new assertions of supremacy on the peoples of western and northern Europe.

Even as that vast social and political transformation began, there were small but significant indications of a very different future, most notably the popular revolts that racked the fourteenth century. Across Europe, urban elites faced repeated disturbance, most dramatically in Florence in 1378, when the Ciompi, ordinary artisans and laborers, briefly took over city government. And France and England saw two major peasant uprisings, the Jacquerie in the 1350s and Jack Cade's Rebellion in the 1380s. These upheavals had little immediate effect, but they remained in the memory. If the age of expanding governmental powers was about to begin, so too was the tradition of popular resistance.

∽◈∽

The assault on the assumptions of medieval philosophy and education is the classic starting point for histories of the Renaissance. If, in the present account, the critique (and eventually the rejection) of the intellectual guidelines of the previous age is treated within a broader context of reaction and change, its importance is nevertheless central. Here is where the confrontation became direct, and where the very notion of a rebirth was formed.

In this story the crucial figure is Petrarch, the most wide-ranging and potent of the assailants of received wisdom and practice during the fourteenth century. His targets ranged from the papacy to poetry, and his vision of the moral life, the goals of learning, and the relation of people to the world around them was to reverberate throughout the Renaissance. That he devised positive guidelines for the future and that his views were to be adopted and elaborated by numerous scholars and propagandists over the next few generations should not, however, cause us to lose sight of his original intention: to put new life into aging conventions. Indeed, Petrarch's protests against the values and institutions of his time and his insistence on better paths to virtue accorded closely with the wider move away from the familiar landmarks of the preceding centuries. Even in his new use of language he was following in the footsteps of the great figure of a generation before, Dante.

Although no summary can do justice to Petrarch's many (and often ambiguous) arguments, those who followed his lead did focus on certain basic contentions. First was the belief, absolutely basic to Renaissance thought, that antiquity provided far more effective and praiseworthy models for human behavior than anything that the intervening centuries had to offer. This was the root of the very conception of the "Middle" Ages, a period when the lessons of ancient societies had been lost. To discover those lessons, it was necessary, second, to bring to light the texts where they could be found—to unearth, and study again, the great writings that had for so long been ignored. Petrarch repeatedly emphasized the need for this encounter, and the letters he wrote to his heroes lamented the decline that separated him from their more glorious days. As he told Livy:

> I would wish either that I had been born in your age, or you in ours. I should thank you, though, that you have so often caused me to forget present evils and have transported me

to happier times. As I read, I seem to be living amidst Scipio, Brutus, and Cato. It is with these men that I live at such times, and not with the thievish company of today, among whom I was born under an evil star.

The recovery of lost meanings required, third, not only a search for texts but also an analysis of their content based on the methods of the scholarly tradition in which Petrarch had been trained, namely, rhetoric. In his view, the effect that words could have was crucial; as he put it, words made "the heart teachable." It was the style as well as the substance of the ancients that had to be imitated. And this led, fourth and finally, to the need for a new kind of education, one centered on the writings of Roman authors such as Cicero. The so-called humanist movement that Petrarch thus founded remained a powerful force in the centuries that followed, though the term *humanist* itself was not contemporary and does not distinsuish Petrarch's disciples from other scholars and writers. Regardless of nomenclature, the issues on which the movement focused—the study of ancient sources, the competition between the active and the contemplative life, the interest in nature, the creation of a system of logic free of medieval dialectic, and in general the need to turn from immediate precedents to the distant past in an effort to improve education, morality, and scholarship itself—became the foundations of Renaissance culture. A revolution in attitude and behavior was about to begin, but it is important to acknowledge that its very purpose was to re-create the past: Uniquely among such movements, it was a backward-looking revolution.

Moreover, the scholastic philosophy that Petrarch derided did not simply fade away. The old continued to flourish alongside the new. Those not headed for a professional career may have gone to humanist schools, but among philosophers and theologians there were probably more trained scholastics than humanists in Europe as late as 1600. Even within this long-standing tradition of theological inquiry and logical argument, though, a new challenge arose in the fourteenth and fifteenth centuries: Against the synthesis of reason and faith trumpeted by the leading lights of the thirteenth century, notably Aquinas, there was posited a philosophy that embraced mystery and the limits of knowledge. Its adherents, known as Nominalists, argued that it was best to keep one's sights low, that grand assertions of general truths were suspect, and that God's ways were unknowable. The most influential exponent of these ideas, William of Ockham (d. 1347), encapsulated the approach in the principle *"Pluralitas non est ponenda sine necessitate"* ("One must not add complexity unnecessarily," often rendered as "The simplest answer is the best answer"). With their suspicion of ambitious claims for reason, the Nominalists offered, in their own way, no less significant a critique of their predecessors than did the humanists or the dissenters from the Church. They were yet another indication of the turning away from the past that animated so much of European society and culture during the 1300s and 1400s.

ఌఓ

The most unmistakable evidence of the break with medieval culture comes from the visual arts. The marked difference that overtook the appearance of buildings, sculptures, and paintings between 1300 and 1500 is, for most people, the essence of the Renaissance. This was cultural shift made visible. Again, it was the deliberate rejection of the immediate past, and a return to antiquity, that spurred the change.

*Fig. 6   The construction of the Milan Cathedral during the 1400s makes it one of the last major buildings completed in the Gothic style. Its complexities contrast sharply with the classical simplicity that Renaissance architects were to seek (see fig. 8).*

Not only can one sense, in such buildings as the Milan Cathedral (begun in 1387 and not completed for more than a century: fig. 6), an over-elaboration of forms that almost invited rejection, but one can also see, in the work of the thirteenth- and early fourteenth-century masters of painting—Duccio, Cimabue, and Giotto—a move toward values different from those that had animated their predecessors. One begins to know the names of artists; one begins to feel stronger emotions in the subjects; one begins to see well-defined landscapes, natural folds in drapery, and three-dimensional figures; and one begins to

*Fig. 7*  The Deposition of Christ, *one of the frescoes Giotto painted in the Arena Chapel in Padua around 1305, reveals the new values appearing in Western art. The interest in the landscape background and the powerful emotions mark a shift in sensibility that was to intensify as artists began to imitate antiquity.*

notice the emphasis on symbolic representation giving way to depictions of recognizable scenes (fig. 7). Petrarch's call to imitate antiquity was but the final summons to seek a new esthetic. Eventually, the name "gothic" was to be applied to medieval art as a term of abuse: an evocation of the "barbarian" Goths.

The admiration for the ancient world ensured that the new artistic styles would echo the broader movements and interests of the new age, and they began with the same kind of dissatisfaction with inherited practice. By the fifteenth century, with the

*Fig. 8   The simple symmetry and classical features of San Lorenzo in Florence, designed by Filippo Brunelleschi and built from the 1420s to the 1460s, makes visible the new esthetics of Renaissance artists as they rejected medieval forms and attempted to revive the style of antiquity.*

work of Van Eyck and his contemporaries in the Netherlands, and the dramatic and deliberate quest for change by Masaccio, Donatello, and Brunelleschi in Florence, the move toward a new esthetic was to accelerate and finally sweep all before it (see plate 1 and figs. 8 and 10). Neither the techniques nor the forms of artistic expression (fig. 9) were to be the same again.

～

The result of the challenges to the past that were mounted (consciously and unconsciously) during the fourteenth and early fifteenth centuries was the overturning of many of the

*Fig. 9　Among the four thousand figures carved in limestone for Chartres Cathedral in the decades around 1200, the calm gravity of the sculptures (exemplified by these saints) that framed the church's three entrances were a particularly important means of conveying to the faithful a reverence for the heroes of the Christian tradition.*

assumptions and conventions that had guided the medieval world. Out of these confrontations, and the struggles that ensued, a new unity of purpose and structure gradually emerged. Although there were, inevitably, large continuities, a distinct

*Fig. 10    Donatello's 1450s wooden sculpture of the repentant Mary Magdalen, clothed in her own hair, is no less an expression of piety than the saints at Chartres (fig. 9); but the rendering of the human form and the Magdalen's intense emotion reflect the new esthetic of the Renaissance.*

set of concerns and conventions was now to bind European society for some three hundred years. Elusive and contradictory though they sometimes were, the major elements of what became a new synthesis of social and cultural commitments can be identified; in the process, it should be possible to define the coherences that held together the age of the Renaissance.

# Chapter Three

# THE CIVILIZATION OF
# THE RENAISSANCE

*E*ver since Jules Michelet and Jacob Burckhardt in the mid-nineteenth century made the case for a distinct Renaissance era in European history, the label has become standard usage for descriptions of the fifteenth and sixteenth centuries. There has been little agreement, however, about the way the period might be defined. So varied have the interpretations been that already in 1948 Wallace Ferguson could devote a book of more than four hundred pages to the ever-changing picture of *The Renaissance in Historical Thought.*

Our concern, however, is not to settle on a definition, but rather to identify (as with the Middle Ages) the distinctive unities of the period: the coherences in thought, creativity, and practice that bound Europe together during a period that extended from the early fifteenth century (when the challenges to the medieval world began to alter that world beyond recognition) to the time when those new bonds themselves began to fray.

The aim, in other words, is to outline those characteristics that distinguished Renaissance Europe from its predecessors and successors. As a result, aspects of the age that came from the past or continued into the future are less central to this inquiry, even though they might have been essential features of the time. Moreover, it is not through a narrative account, but through a series of cross-sections, that we will be able to identify what set the Renaissance apart.

⁓

Gunpowder warfare was the most unprecedented of the new circumstances that shaped the Renaissance, even though the change in weaponry was at first a slow process. The explosive potential of a mixture of sulphur, charcoal, and potassium nitrate (known as saltpeter) seems first to have been recognized in Europe during the fourteenth century—in the earliest days of the Renaissance as defined here. Its use for destructive purposes gained wide acceptance only gradually, however, mainly because it was so difficult to control. The earliest applications required the manufacture of long metal tubes through which projectiles could be hurled with great force by gunpowder explosions. These cannon were often as dangerous to their dischargers as to their targets. Moreover, a lack of standardization in their construction, not to mention the haphazard shapes of projectiles, meant that accuracy was minimal (fig. 11). When they were fired, balls of varied shapes and sizes would bounce off the walls of cannon and emerge at unpredictable angles. As a result, these early weapons terrified an enemy more by the

*Fig. 11 An anonymous German woodcut of the 1520s suggests the astonishing variety of cannon that were manufactured in an age before standardization. These highly decorated examples, however, would have been made on special commission.*

noise they made and the smoke they produced than by the damage they inflicted.

Nevertheless, during the next century gunpowder established itself as the dominant instrument in the waging of war, and its unrestrained advance is one of the defining marks of Renaissance Europe. The attempts that eventually were made to limit its effects are a sure sign that the world of the Renaissance was coming to an end. Until that turnaround began, the ingenuity of the armaments experts in devising multiple shot, cannonballs with chains, and other such instruments of gory death ensured that cannon and the missiles they dispatched became ever more dependable and devastating. At the same time, new and constantly improved forms of weaponry— portable guns, hand guns, lightweight cannon, mines—multiplied the effects of the original discovery in every arena of combat.

The effects of these inventions, and of the costly measures taken by armies and governments to exploit them, spread throughout society. As new industries arose to produce the weapons, so older ones expanded to meet changing conditions. Thus, when gunpowder made medieval walls and castles obsolete, the building of massive defensive walls and bastions became a high priority throughout Europe. It has been said that making or laying bricks was the most secure trade of the sixteenth and seventeenth centuries. And it was not only the armament and construction industries that were affected.

Military leaders soon realized that, because a gunner could be trained fairly easily (certainly by comparison with a mounted knight or a longbowman) and equipped relatively cheaply, armies could grow exponentially. Battle were won and sieges brought to successful conclusions only to some extent because of better tactics and discipline. Above all, firepower had to be maximized; cavalry, infantry, and garrisons alike could be overwhelmed by superior forces of guns and cannon. The result was an enormous increase in the size of armies. Henry V probably had no more than 6,000 to 8,000 men at Agincourt in 1415. By the late seventeenth century, Louis XIV kept 400,000 men permanently under arms. And for every soldier there were something like five people in support positions: bakers, tentmakers, surgeons, carters, blacksmiths, camp followers, and so forth. Sieges became massive operations, because the only way attackers could breach ten-foot-thick walls

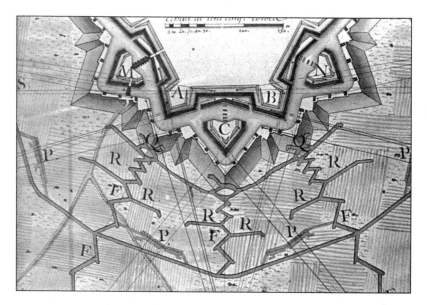

*Fig. 12    The greatest fortification expert of the seventeenth century, Louis XIV's Marshal Sébastien Vauban, designed bastions and siege works. This pattern of trenches for a siege indicates how complex and wearying even a gunpowder assault could be.*

was to set off an explosion at their base, and to get to the walls while avoiding defensive fire from bastions they had to dig elaborate networks of trenches that required long and back-breaking labor (fig. 12). If one adds to the equation naval construction, which was also transformed by gunpowder (as commanders realized that sinking a ship with firepower was more effective than trying to capture it), and the cost of administering this gigantic effort of recruitment, training, and supply, it is no surprise that military expenditures dominated government finances during these centuries. And if the opportunities for employment mushroomed, so too did the social and economic dislocations as troops appropriated supplies and people from the territories they traversed.

Scholars differ as to whether all this constituted a revolution, and if it did, when it began and whether it was mainly a matter of technology or tactics, of social impact or political direction. Regardless of interpretation, though, there is no mistaking the rapid and unrelenting growth, from the mid-1400s until the mid-1600s, in the size of armies, in the outlays they demanded, and in the casualties they inflicted. Europe had not seen this scale of warfare since the glory days of the Roman Empire, and it had *never* seen such destructive power.

∽

No less revolutionary than the upheaval in warfare was the concomitant transformation of politics, usually described as state-building. This was an intensive, though not universal, process that swept through smaller principalities as well as large territorial states. It entailed the centralization of power, extensive bureaucratization, rapidly rising taxes, a major expansion of war-making capacities, and—particularly distinctive—the gradual integration (or "domestication") of traditionally independent authorities, notably aristocracies, into the mechanisms of the state. This last element worked as both cause and symptom of a shift in social and political authority from the locality to the center, and it helped create a further novelty: a system of international relations that overturned the non-state-oriented commitments (such as loyalty to the Church) that previously had played a major role in princes' dealings with one another.

The origins of this transformation of politics can be traced to various pressures, but foremost was the explosive growth in the magnitude and costs of warfare. The expenses now involved in outfitting an army and building massive defense works meant that the traditional great lord in his castle, surrounded by his retainers, could no longer maintain his military independence. Fielding an effective fighting force demanded a level of resources, authority, and administrative capacity that only an organized territorial state could achieve. But the state, too, had to reform its structure and practices if it was to meet the challenge of gunpowder conflict.

Historians have long debated whether the expansion of warfare caused the expansion of the state or vice versa. Since the argument for war relies on the impact of an unforeseen new influence, gunpowder, however, it seems plausible to tilt the balance in that direction. But whatever the principal engine of change, the two processes were intimately connected. Neither is conceivable without the other.

Indeed, there is little doubt that the chief reason a Renaissance prince sought new financial resources and hired more officials—the activities that were the essence of state-building—was to wage war more effectively. Whether it was the ruler of a small territory, such as the Medici in Florence or the Wittelsbachs in Bavaria, or a great king such as Philip II of Spain or Louis XIV of France, the driving justification for the growth of budgets and bureaucracies was the need to finance and administer armies and navies.

The result was not only a rise in taxes and widespread bureaucratization, but also, inevitably, a centralization of political decisionmaking and control. In the states where offices were sold to raise money, the surge in taxes and the spread of bureaucracy were particularly closely linked; but everywhere rulers embraced military and political ambitions that fueled these developments (fig. 13). Between the fourteenth and seventeenth centuries, as a

*Fig. 13 That the Flemish painter Reymerswaele portrayed tax collectors several times (this 1549 painting emphasizes their wealth and grasping natures) reflects the growing intrusion of officialdom into daily life.*

result, territorial states began to take shape throughout Europe, creating institutions, systems of control, and loyalties that laid the foundations for the modern state.

Symptomatic of this change was the emergence of the word "state" into normal usage around 1600. As students of political thought have noted, this was the period when, for the first time, the state came to be defined as an impersonal presence, with a life that was independent both of the people who were its members and of the government that ruled it (a similar impersonality descended on the business corporation at the same time). The Italian Niccolò Machiavelli in the early sixteenth century set politics apart as a separate realm of inquiry, but his successors throughout Europe—notably Francisco de Vitoria, Jean Bodin, Hugo Grotius, and Thomas Hobbes, in Spain, France, the Netherlands, and England, respectively—went much further. They not only created notions of Natural Law that superseded the specific interests of particular countries or regions but also devised geographical and historical analyses that removed the state from its personal and divine moorings. Even though claims of proprietary dynasticism—the belief that the state *belonged* to a ruling house, famously summed up by Lous XIV as "L'État, c'est moi"—persisted, the impersonality of the state also began to penetrate the thinking of statesmen. Thus, Cardinal Richelieu, ruler of France in the second quarter of the seventeenth century, could treat politics in his *Testament Politique* as a distinct realm: The state itself, not particular princes, had to ensure that its interests were always served.

In one important respect, the Renaissance phase of this long-term transformation of the political landscape was unique. There were three redoubtable rivals to the authority of princes and kings at the end of the Middle Ages: the Church, the independent city, and the aristocracy. What was distinct about the story of state-building during this period was that between the fourteenth and the seventeenth centuries these three rivals were vanquished.

Although central governments still faced many problems when they tried to impose their will on regions or subjects in 1700, the ecclesiastics, townsmen, and nobles who had been the chief sources of alternative authority three hundred years earlier had by and large been tamed. The victory over these competing powers was essential to the future advance of state-building, and it was during the Renaissance that it was won.

Where the Church was concerned, the Reformation proved crucial. For Protestant rulers, it was an opportunity to subordinate the spiritual realm to the needs of the state—either by minimizing ecclesiastical influence or, more dramatically, by wholesale appropriation. In England, for instance, when Henry VIII dissolved his country's allegiance to the pope, he had his Parliament proclaim a formal act in 1534 that was unequivocal:

> Albeit, the King's Majesty justly and rightfully is and oweth [ought] to be the supreme head of the Church of England, and so is recognised by the clergy of this realm in their Convocations; yet nevertheless for corroboration and confirmation thereof, and for increase of virtue in Christ's religion within this realm of England, and to repress and extirp all errors, heresies and other enormities and abuses heretofore used in the same, Be it enacted by authority of this present Parliament that the King our sovereign lord, his heirs and successors kings of this realm, shall be taken, accepted and reputed the only supreme head in earth of the Church of England.

Secure in his authority, Henry went on to dissolve England's monasteries and confiscate their wealth.

For Catholics, the religious struggles of the sixteenth century were equally the occasion for princes to assert their power. Rulers were now essential to the defense of the faith, and in regimes as different as those of Spain, France, or Bohemia, they were able to make the Church serve their own ends. Many reversed the outcome of the investiture dispute of the thirteenth century and regained control over the appointment of bishops. Smaller powers such as the Wittelsbachs of Bavaria, on the other hand, parlayed their loyalty to Rome (and the papacy's need for a secure princely ally in Germany) to gain lucrative Church positions for members of the family. This was not entirely a one-sided relationship. When, during the Thirty Years' War, the Wittelsbach duke, Maximilian of Bavaria, tried to pursue a self-serving foreign policy that clashed with Church interests, Rome dispatched a remarkable Capuchin friar, Father Hyacinth, to his court. Father Hyacinth would sit down in the main entranceway, refuse all food, and swear that he would starve himself to death if the duke did not change course. To such blackmail Maximilian had to give in, although as the decades went by (he was duke for more than fifty years) he acted with increasing independence. The full extent of the triumph of the Catholic princes became apparent when Pope Innocent X denounced the Treaties of Westphalia that ended the Thirty Years War in 1648, but Catholic rulers paid as little heed as the Protestants to the papacy's views.

Part of this process was the "desacralization" of kings. Although monarchs continued to be anointed with holy oil at their coronations, their identification as instruments of divine grace gradually receded. Louis XIV's authority in the late seventeenth century may have been justified by Bishop Bossuet from "the very words of scripture," but the king himself saw the pagan god Apollo as his model and took the sun as his symbol. His contemporary as ruler of Britain, Queen Anne, brought to an end the centuries-old tradition of believing that the "royal touch," powered by divine grace, could heal sufferers from scrofula.

The subjugation of cities, many of which had enjoyed long traditions of self-government and independence, was more straightforward. Despite their wealth and influence, they could not resist the resources, the bureaucratic weight, or the military might of centralizing princes. Venice and Geneva were exceptions that proved the rule: Venice because she herself ruled an empire, Geneva because her vast hinterland was international Calvinism. Elsewhere, proud cities such as Florence or Genoa became pawns in the hands of powerful princes. And a final burst of resistance in the mid-seventeenth century, when such different places as Barcelona, Bordeaux, Paris, London, Amsterdam, and Königsberg all revolted against their rulers, only to be crushed and integrated into large territorial states, merely demonstrated that the autonomy they had once enjoyed was irrevocably lost. Theorists liked to see these cities as embodiments of republican virtue, reminiscent of the Roman Republic and superior in their liberties to heavy-handed principalities and kingdoms. But events such as the crushing of the Ciompi revolt in Florence show that urban oligarchs were usually no less repressive than monarchs, and the absorption of cities during the state-building process is unlikely to have diminished significantly their residents' sense of political openness.

The taming of aristocracies was more difficult. Here the task was not so much to subjugate as to co-opt, a far more challenging enterprise. There was no way a prince could gain control of a state without the active help of the nobility that had controlled local areas for centuries. A genuine partnership was needed, not obedience or grudging cooperation. Only with the help of those who dominated the countryside could a ruler hope to exercise authority throughout his realm.

The first indications of the effectiveness of such a system had been seen in late medieval England, where the great men of the counties gradually undertook, through unpaid administrative offices and by attendance at Parliament, to help unite the country behind the decisions of its central government. Not until a bitter civil war in the mid-seventeenth century, however, when it became clear how dangerous it was for one side to ignore the other, were the partners fully convinced that they had to work together.

Similar alliances were achieved at about the same time in other European states. Whether the outcome was a structure built around the "absolute" powers of a monarch—such as Louis XIV in France, Emperor Leopold I in Vienna, or Charles II in Spain—or a parliamentary or republican system such as arose in England and the Netherlands, the basic alliance between governments and local leaders was essential to the success of centralization. By taking on the leadership of a state's army and bureaucracy, Europe's aristocrats achieved levels of influence and power that they had never been able to attain in their localities alone, where they had focused on defending their ancient rights and resisting the encroachment of princes. And their rulers, in turn, gained the vital assistance of those most capable of exercising military and political leadership on behalf of the state. It was a partnership that resolved the struggle between center and regions that had dominated Europe for centuries, and it proved to be a crucial phase in the development of the modern state.

Especially noteworthy was the creation of a quite distinct republican political tradition. Its roots grew in a handful of prosperous and relatively independent cities in the late Middle

Ages, and it drew inspiration from the memory of Republican Rome, but it began to flower only in the fourteenth and subsequent centuries. As most of the cities where it began declined in importance, its main exemplars were to be found in Venice, Switzerland, the Netherlands, and Oliver Cromwell's British Isles. These regimes may have been oligarchies, but many did make room for elections by limited constituencies, and they all emphasized the "liberties" of their citizens in contrast to the "subject" status of those who were ruled by hereditary princes. In the long run, their ideas were to be superseded by the far more embracing notions of republican and democratic government that arose in the eighteenth century, but they nevertheless helped prepare the way, during this era, for the later developments that were to be so crucial in shaping modern political structures.

There were two other aspects of Renaissance state-building that set this period apart. First, visible and dramatic, was the Turkish threat. This unique confrontation in European history is almost coterminous with the Renaissance. If the capture of Constantinople by the Ottomans in 1453 has sometimes been treated as the opening date of the era, then certainly the failure of their second siege of Vienna in 1683 marks the end. For 230 years, Europe lived in constant fear of its neighbor to the east; the opening up of Vienna and the Habsburg reconquest of the Balkans after 1683 were both marks of the new sense of confidence in Europe's states.

In addition, the very consolidation of territorial regimes meant that their dealings with one another had to be systematized. From tentative beginnings on the Italian peninsula, an elaborate network of diplomatic connections and procedures took hold throughout Europe. Between the peace of Lodi in

1454 and the peace of Westphalia in 1648, not only were new ways devised for princes to negotiate with one another but a new profession, diplomacy, was born. It is notable that one of the shrewdest observers of this process, Cardinal Richelieu, recommended in his *Testament Politique* that princes should always be negotiating; otherwise, they would miss opportunities and fail to detect shifts in the diplomatic winds. And the result was clear. In the treaties of 1648, a large proportion of the continent's territorial states tried for the first time to solve in one sweep as many of their outstanding differences as possible. Only the successes of state-building allowed them to move beyond the resolution of specific, immediate conflicts—the goal of all previous peace conferences, which had usually involved no more than two or three interested parties—and begin to create a large-scale system of international relations.

∽

A fundamental prerequisite for the new role Europe's traditional elite played in state-building was the transformation of their basic outlook and behavior that has been called the "domestication" of the aristocracy. This was an intellectual, social, and political reorientation—the creation of a new self-image—that was closely associated with the larger cultural ideals of the Renaissance.

In the late Middle Ages, the nobleman was regarded essentially as a warrior. What set the elite apart was its special place in battle. Although the cult of courtly love encouraged attention to peaceful pursuits, and the knightly ideal was intertwined with religious commitments, the basic quality that distinguished the lord was his bravery and skill in armed conflict. To that end, the equipment and training that made his military role possible—his castle, his armor, his horse, his right to command—was supported by the entire community. Nowhere within that definition, however, was there a notion of refinement, cultural accomplishment (the likelihood that he could read and write was remote), or superiority in intellect, taste, and style.

All of that was transformed in the Renaissance. As secular learning and the arts became the source of a new kind of prestige (noticeably in Italy in the fourteenth century, but soon thereafter in most areas), aristocrats' ambitions changed accordingly. By the early 1500s, the shifts in their outlook were being fashioned into a new code of conduct.

The change was made imperative by the newly impersonal destructiveness of gunpowder. Death was now dealt at a distance, and it therefore became almost impossible to sustain the quality that, for centuries, had set the noble knight apart: his valor. Already by 1516, in his widely read epic *Orlando Furioso*, Ludovico Ariosto felt compelled to lament the changing standards of battlefield honor that were the result of the new weaponry. In a famous episode in Canto XI, his hero, Orlando, tosses a cannon into the sea with the words:

> *How, foul and pestilent discovery,*
> *Didst thou find place within the human heart?*
> *Through thee is martial glory lost;*
> *Through thee the trade of arms became a worthless art:*
> *And at such ebb are worth and chivalry,*
> *That the base often plays the better part.*
> *Through thee no more shall gallantry, no more*
> *Shall valour, prove their prowess as of yore.*

Ninety years later, that sentiment was echoed by Europe's last great knight, Cervantes' Don Quixote:

> Blessed be those happy ages that were strangers to the dreadful fury of these devilish instruments of artillery, whose inventor I am satisfied is now in Hell, receiving the reward of his cursed invention, which is the cause that very often a cowardly base hand takes away the life of the bravest gentleman.

At almost exactly the same time as Ariosto was writing, another Italian, Baldassare Castiglione, was offering a much broader response to the erosion that he observed in the traditional military justification for nobility. Confronted with the collapse of the brilliant Italian city-states at the hands of French and Habsburg armies—the foreign "barbarians" who so distressed another contemporary, Niccolò Machiavelli—Castiglione came up with a new justification for the superiority of the aristocrat. If military skill no longer made Italian nobles distinct, either from their own subjects or from their peers elsewhere, new claims had to be made for their preeminence. The eponymous hero of the book in which Castiglione laid out the new standards of behavior, *The Courtier,* might still have excelled at arms, but now it was no less important that he be accomplished in arts and letters, and that he display taste, decorum, elegance, and refinement. Indeed, the book's chief spokesman, the Count, affirmed that "it is not so necessary for any man to be learned, as it is for a man of war." Cultivation, Castiglione argued, sets the gentleman apart as surely as his valor, and this prescription soon established a new norm for Europe's elite.

*Fig. 14   Pedro Berruguete's 1480 portrait of the ruler of Urbino, Federigo da Montefeltro, and his son encapsulates the cultural shift as the nobility began to value learning as much as war.*

With warfare thus democratized, only jousting and duels offered opportunities for traditional, chivalric displays of noble virtue. These events survived well into the sixteenth century, but it was as a last gesture toward a dying ideal that the decoration of Henry VIII's palace at Hampton Court presented an iconographic scheme of heroism-and-holiness that its historian has described as "a never-never land of chivalric values" encompassing Hercules, Abraham, King Arthur, Julius Caesar, and King David. As bravery lost its glow, the joys of patronage helped to create a new style of life. One has but to look at the

*Fig. 15 The same year as the equestrian portrait (plate 4), Titian also painted Charles V as a fine gentleman, seated and thoughtful, in front of a gentle landscape. The contrast suggests Charles's greatness in peace as well as war.*

evolution of the portrait to see the revolution in self-image unfold. Duke Federigo of Urbino, called "the light of Italy" by Castiglione, made the point visible by having himself portrayed sitting in front of a lectern in full armor, but reading a book (fig. 14). The supreme lord of the age, the Emperor Charles V, appeared in Titian's portraits both as a Christian knight on horseback (plate 4) and as a gentleman peacefully seated in a chair (fig. 15). A century later, Charles I of England could still be seen in both guises in paintings by van Dyck (fig. 16 and plate 7). When, however, the artist represented two cousins of

*Fig. 16 Nearly a century after Titian's prototype (plate 4), van Dyck in 1637 painted the far more pacific Charles I of England in the same pose, as a glorious mounted knight in full armor. But see plate 7.*

the king, Lord John and Lord Bernard Stuart, he showed them, not as the soldiers they were, soon to die in battle, but rather as gorgeously attired, disdainful exemplars (almost caricatures) of Castiglione's courtier (fig. 17). Other forces were at work, notably the prestige that Renaissance culture conferred on the discriminating patron, but there is no doubt that one of the chief reasons the gentleman forged a new image for himself was the need to come to terms with the changing demands of gunpowder warfare. It could help him sustain his status *only* if fame could be achieved as effectively through portraits and book dedications as on the battlefield.

*Fig. 17 Van Dyck's 1637 portrait of Lords John and Bernard Stuart, cousins of the king, shows the new image of the aristocracy at its height. The brothers were in fact soldiers, to be killed in England's civil wars, but they wished to be seen, not as valorous, but in rich attire and in almost excessively elegant and condescending poses.*

But there were other changes as well. If esthetic sensibilities could become a mark of the fine gentleman, so too could the skills of the administrator. With written records and complex markets proliferating, the great landowners had ever more need of numeracy as well as literacy to run successful estates. They came increasingly to prize education for themselves and their heirs, sending their sons to universities in unprecedented numbers; at the same time, they pursued their new interests by launching a remarkable surge of townhouse construction. Never before had the aristocracy owned so many homes near the centers of culture and power in cities such as Paris and London; and when the owners were in town, their proximity to one another created a new phenomenon, the social "season." Having thus paved the way intellectually and geographically, Europe's nobles by the mid-seventeenth century were primed for their new role in state-building. Ready to serve central governments as once they had served their localities, they completed a reorientation of purpose and esteem that would have astonished their ancestors of three centuries before.

⚘

None of the defining features of the Renaissance had a more profound impact on the future than the massive overseas conquests and migrations of these centuries. Starting with the Portuguese capture of Ceuta in North Africa in 1415, and made possible by the spread of new instruments such as the compass, this was a movement of peoples that reversed millennia of migration into Europe. Alexander's armies and the Crusaders had made brief forays toward the East, but few of the invaders remained in the lands they had overrun. From the fifteenth century onward, however, the transfer of population into Asia and across the Atlantic reached hitherto unparalleled levels. It has been estimated that, by 1700, some 1 million Europeans lived overseas (roughly one for every thirty inhabitants in the countries from which most had come). Many more had set out, but had perished en route.

Significantly, it was during this period that the word *Europe* began to take on its modern meaning. Although the term had long existed, as a self-defining collectivity it replaced the term *Christendom* only during the Renaissance. As one historian has noted, when Francis Bacon spoke of "we Europeans" in 1623, he was using a phrase that probably would have made little sense to his readers 150 years earlier. There could hardly be a better indication of the revolution wrought in self-consciousness as well as in the continent's relations with the rest of the world than this change in language. The new meaning was accompanied, moreover, by an entirely new way of picturing the vast spaces that travelers crossed: For the first time, mapmakers used surveyors' tools and refined mathematical techniques to create accurate representations (not symbolic ones, as in the Middle Ages) of the shapes and dimensions of lands and oceans.

Territorial expansion also impelled to new heights the xenophobia that had been unwavering ever since the invention of "barbarians" in ancient Greece. The violent mistreatment of native populations, and the exponential increase in the enslavement of Africans, marked a new phase in relations with non-Europeans.

⌇⋙

Of the new directions in European culture and society that took shape during the Renaissance, few have had as contested a history as the rise of capitalism. It is not just that early stirrings of the practices and attitudes that the word denotes can be spotted in medieval cities. Even the most enthusiastic advocate of gradual and almost invisible development in human affairs will admit that, after the fourteenth century, a new stage was reached: the establishment of the market as the basic institution of Europe's economic life. But acknowledgment of this "commercialization," as it is often called, does not end the arguments over definition and chronology, arguments that to some degree remain fraught because of the persistent shadow of Karl Marx.

Even without the ideological implications that lurk behind every statement on the subject, there is little agreement about the relative importance of the three principal interpretations that have been put forward during the past 150 years. The first is the emphasis on markets. A capitalist system was put into place, in this view, when transactions became monetarized, the marketplace controlled economic behavior, supply and demand rather than the "just price" determined wages and prices, and goods and services were exchanged relatively freely. The process did not advance at the same pace in all areas, and debate continues about its penetration of the countryside; but in this increasingly urbanized society there can be little doubt that, by the seventeenth century, capitalism, as so defined, dominated Europe's economy. The indices of that triumph—the rapid growth of cities, perhaps twenty of them exceeding 50,000 inhabitants, and London and Paris exceeding five times that number, by 1700; the spread of the "putting-out" system, which created a division of labor and a new set of economic relations in the manufacture of cloth and textiles; the widespread acceptance of new financial institutions such as banks and stock exchanges; and the accelerating recognition of the importance of the impersonal business enterprise and the needs of the commercial community—were visible throughout Europe (fig. 18). If this be capitalism, there is no question that the Renaissance witnessed its creation.

A second interpretation emphasizes mental state. It is the outlook of the capitalist, rather than the institutions and patterns within which he operated, that is decisive. Unlike the bazaar merchant, who closed his shop as soon as he had earned enough for dinner (to put the distinction in its simplest form), his more disciplined successor stayed on to make a profit that

*Fig. 18   Jost Amman's woodcuts for a 1568 Book of Trades,* Das Ständebuch, *offer some of the first visualizations of the retail and manufacturing activities of an increasingly prosperous and capitalist economy. Oil production, as we see here, still relied on horse and grindstone, but the demand for labor meant that it employed women as well as men.*

he could reinvest in his business. Sober judgment, long-term planning, careful record keeping, rational pursuit of sustained profit—these are the marks of the capitalist (fig. 19). Without the right attitude, the system as a whole could not have been put into place. Those who take this approach usually emphasize spirit rather than structure, but they would agree that the era of the Renaissance was when the new behavior took hold.

The same is true of the third line of argument, associated with Marx, which highlights the social relations of the actors in the drama. The engine of change here is the bourgeoisie, the determined and entrepreneurial urban class, inferior to the landowning elite, but relentless in its pursuit of wealth. To achieve

*Fig. 19 Possibly a portrait of St. Eligius, the patron saint of metalworkers, this 1449 painting by Petrus Christus brings to life the reviving Netherlandish economy of the age. We see a goldsmith's shop, its rich clientele, elaborate goods for sale, and its urban setting in the mirror.*

its ends, it exploits the labor of those who produce the basic goods that society needs, such as bricks and clothing, rope and pottery—that is, the working class, which is essentially propertyless—while maintaining its ownership of the means of production.

However the system is defined, though, whether as market, outlook, or class exploitation, the inescapable conclusion is that it came into being during the Renaissance, and that it is one of the defining characteristics of the age. Nor is there any doubt that contemporaries noticed what was happening. Since Shakespeare commented on just about every major issue that his society confronted, it is no surprise that, despite the word not having been

*Fig. 20 The growing impor- tance of the mone- tary economy, and the qualities it en- couraged, made it an increasingly common subject for artists. Sobriety, painstaking care, and accuracy are conveyed in this 1514 portrait by Quentin Metsys of a money lender, his literate wife, and their client reflected in the mirror.*

invented, he wrote a play *(The Merchant of Venice)* about capital- ism and set it in Venice, capitalism's quintessential home.

～

It was in urban centers that the effects of the behaviors and at- titudes associated with capitalism were most visible (fig. 20). Yet one cannot argue that the city itself was a Renaissance in- vention. It had existed for millennia. Its structure and organiza- tion within the European context, moreover, was distinguished from its medieval predecessor only in two ways: size and ser- vices. Numbers grew so substantially that urbanization reached a level not seen since antiquity. But that was mainly a matter of scale. More immediately apparent were the development of innovative administrative mechanisms such as the control of plague and the distribution of water, developments that increasingly persuaded citizens to look to municipal governments, rather than to guilds, in matters of governance and welfare. The consequent decline of the guilds marked a major shift in the organization of urban life.

During this period, too, the notion of a capital city was first fully defined. Previously, even such dominant cities as London and Paris had lost preeminence when kings spent time elsewhere. But by 1700, even if the court was nearby—at Windsor or Versailles, for example—there was no doubt as to the state's administrative capital. That so many of the capitals that are familiar to this day (Stockholm, Berlin, Vienna, Madrid) discovered their roles during the Renaissance merely confirms how widespread was the process of definition that was underway.

In one crucial respect, however, apart from the growing prominence throughout European society of urban centers, and the spread (even beyond towns) of the capitalist mentality that they fostered, the city gained unprecedented recognition. For the first time artists, geometers, and geographers learned how to depict the configuration and fabric of urban spaces. The consequence was the creation of a distinctive era in the history of the city: the transformation of its self-image. The invention of the map as we know it, with all the attendant issues of projecting a sphere onto a flat surface, can be regarded as a consequence of Europe's overseas expansion, or else as a part of the scientific revolution that will be addressed below; but this major landmark of the period was not merely a reflection of other forces. The change it wrought in the way people perceived the physical world had consequences of its own.

Where the city is concerned, that effect was connected to the simultaneous but separate development of perspective as a means of representing the visible. This advance is particularly pertinent to the revolution in the art of painting during the fifteenth century, but it also helped define a major subdiscipline within mapmaking: the perspectival cityscape. By making possible the detailed city survey and city plan, these two visual breakthroughs had as much influence on the definition of urban life as they did on the development of new forms of art and academic learning.

The result was not only a godsend for those who established new features and new districts in Europe's cities (an enterprise that assumed ever-larger ambitions during this period, especially as aristocrats carved out newly fashionable areas for their town houses), but also a means for both governments and citizens to understand the habitats in which they lived. It is no coincidence that Philip II of Spain, the most powerful king of the second half of the sixteenth century, commissioned views of the cities he ruled as he regularized and bureaucratized the techniques of government. These overviews and plans came to be popular projects for governments as well as collectors' items for the patriotically or scientifically inclined. Where the *Nuremberg Chronicle* of 1493 included woodcuts of cities as an added feature, with some charming notions of famous sights (e.g., the Pantheon in Rome), just seven years later the famous Barbari map of Venice was setting new standards of accuracy in portraying a city (figs. 21 and 22).

This increased attention to the fidelity of depiction created an understanding of the nature of the city that previously had been unavailable. Books about cities, such as John Stow's *Survey of London* (1598), found a ready market, as did the gigantic

*Fig. 21    A detail of the woodcut depiction of Rome in the 1493* Nuremberg Chronicle *shows the symbolic representation of cities (the main landmark here is the Pantheon), which was about to give way to the careful reproduction of urban landscapes characteristic of the sixteenth century (fig. 22).*

and expensive birds'-eye scenes of cities and battles that were produced by Jacques Callot in the 1620s. For the first time, urban dwellers had access to a lifelike image of the larger context in which they had made their homes. To the extent that the city

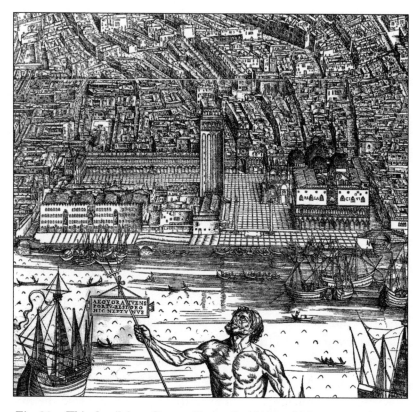

*Fig. 22   This detail from Jacopo Barbari's 1500 multisheet engraving of a bird's-eye view of Venice, in which almost every building can be identified, was the result of painstaking observation from bell towers and a wish to depict a recognizable, not symbolic, city.*

did not finally become a fully rounded concept in people's minds until they could picture it fairly precisely, that final step was not taken until the Renaissance.

The theme of capitalism ascendant is applicable not only to the cities where it began and most obviously flourished but also to the rural world. As the above reference to the "putting-out" system may indicate, the intrusion of new economic practices into the countryside was yet another of the distinctive features of the age. "Putting-out," or "domestic industry," encouraged a specialization of functions that turned entire villages into way stations along the route of Europe's largest manufacturing effort, the production of cloth. Organized into coherent regional systems, usually by entrepreneurs in nearby towns or cities, wool and cloth producers in an increasing number of the major sheep-raising territories of northern Europe began to take on differentiated roles. Where once a village might have started with its sheep, sheared them, and then taken the wool through all the required processes until it had manufactured cloth, now the different processes were disaggregated so as to create specialization and efficiency of scale. Thus one area might do nothing but raise and shear sheep, another might focus on dyeing, another on fulling, and so forth. Drawn into the orbit of the entrepreneur who supplied the materials and sold the finished product, these inhabitants of the countryside were as affected by the growing force of commercialization as were their contemporaries in the city.

And there were other ways in which an old order was passing. The devastations of the Black Death and recurrent plagues and famines certainly caused serious hardship, possibly as a result of a "little ice age" that some climatologists (though not all) suggest might have begun around 1400. But the shrinking population of the fourteenth and much of the fifteenth century also made labor far more valuable, and at least west of the Elbe River it brought serfdom to an end. Equally important, the economic and demographic changes that disrupted the traditional homogeneity of the village led to higher rates of migration and a growing disparity of wealth between those able to take advantage of the new conditions (especially when a rising population began to need ever more food) and those who did not. It is significant that, by the end of the seventeenth century, the councils of local elders that had been a common sight in European villages, overseeing daily concerns, mediating disputes, and in general acting as a trusted point of reference within the community, had virtually ceased to exist.

The commercialization of the countryside did not move at the same pace in all regions. Its effects were most sharply felt in the principal wool-growing and textile-producing areas of northern Europe (centers of the "putting-out" system) and in northern Italy. The saying "Seek a weaver and you will find a heretic" that became common during the Reformation was a reflection of the dislocations and unease in this most fundamental of industries. But the growth of cities and the marshalling of the areas that surrounded them to meet their needs—for food, goods, and manpower—had the same effects. Migration, and the widening divide between those who prospered and those who did not, undermined traditional social relations in many areas.

This erosion used to be described as the progression from one social configuration to another, both encapsulated in the German terms *Gemeinschaft* and *Gesellschaft* (community and society, or social homogeneity and differention). Although the terms are now rarely used—partly because these were often not distinct situations, partly because the process went through many stages, and partly because they implied that the second was an improvement on the first—they do suggest how commercialization altered rural life. That it was during the Renaissance that this process got under way is another of the period's defining attributes.

⸎

Perhaps the most clear-cut boundary marker of the Renaissance was the bubonic plague that first struck Europe in the 1340s and did not die out as a recurrent scourge until the late 1600s and early 1700s. What began as a deadly disease that ravaged Europe in the fourteenth century and killed perhaps one third of its inhabitants, settled down thereafter to lesser but still ruinous reappearances. At least once every generation, an outbreak carried off disproportionately the old and the very young. When it struck an area, it exacerbated the bad harvests that also recurred at regular intervals, triggering subsistence crises that caused alarming swings in mortality. One of the markers of the end of the Renaissance was the disappearance of bubonic plague as a periodic visitor in the West.

The reasons that Europe's population began to grow again in the late fifteenth century, after more than a hundred years of loss and stagnation, remain elusive. It has been suggested that a warming climate could have improved agricultural yields until a "little ice age" of lowered temperatures in the seventeenth century (which most climatologists *do* accept) led to a new period of stagnation. There is also evidence that longer intervals between outbreaks after 1500 weakened the virulence of the plague. On the other hand, the ever-widening effects of warfare in the sixteenth century, which often was as destructive as plague or famine when an army traversed a region, ought to have undermined whatever gains were made. Regardless of the reasons for the demographic patterns, however, the aura of plague and famine that hung over these centuries remained one of the most distinctive features of the age.

⤳

Thus far, our emphasis has been on the coherences of the Renaissance that are visible in its political, economic, and social organizations. We now come to the commitment that has more commonly been seen as the chief distinguishing mark of the age: the turn to the distant past. Although the context presented here is broader, one cannot diminish the importance, indeed the centrality, of this feature of Europe's literate culture. After all, it has given the period its name.

That Petrarch is often called the Father of the Renaissance is not inappropriate. His momentous decision to look to the distant past for guidance lent his distaste for his own times and the "Middle" Ages, as well as his urgent quest to define the virtuous life, a resonance that long outlived him. The solution that Petrarch found in antiquity, where men such as Cicero had, in his view, combined disinterested public service with a private quest for the highest moral standards, created an entire Renaissance genre: a debate about the contemplative versus the active life. Although he was troubled that the Romans were not Christians, this did not deter him or his followers from imitating their example. Petrarch himself was a diplomat as well as a poet, and in the generations that followed the idea took hold (notably in the Florentine movement known as civic humanism) that the highest virtue could be achieved only by seeking the benefit of the community as well as personal betterment.

Petrarch's call for backward-looking reform caught fire, first in his native Florence, then throughout Italy, and eventually in all of Europe. As a result, the "humanist" passions that he unleashed—the obsessive recovery and study of ancient texts, the insistence on a mastery of perfect Latin and its use for the attainment of eloquence—swept through princely courts, schools, and universities and became the mark of an educated person. Petrarch himself emphasized the more familiar heritage of Rome, but ancient Greece also came to the fore after the capture of Constantinople by the Ottomans and the exodus of Byzantine scholars to Italy. The ensuing admiration for Plato added a new level of reverence for antiquity through the ever-widening influence of its otherworldly and Christianized variant, Neoplatonism. Eventually, the humanists, particularly those working in the north of Europe, such as Erasmus, made Christian antiquity no less than pagan antiquity the focus of their research and their admiration.

These imitations and evocations of the ancient world had far-reaching consequences for education, literature, the arts, religion, and political thought. And they remained an unshakeable model for the literate classes throughout the ensuing three centuries and beyond.

The most tangible evidence of their impact comes from the visual arts, where the innovations of Brunelleschi, Masaccio, and Donatello in Florence in the early fifteenth century, inspired by Petrarch's call to study the ancients, created a new esthetic that carried all before it. Within a few generations, Botticelli could paint an ancient mythological scene, such as the *Birth of Venus,* exactly as he imagined a Roman would have painted it (plate 2). Michelangelo could equal the genius of the ancient sculptor of the Laocoön—a statue unearthed in Rome, to enormous excitement, in the early sixteenth century—and design a dome (for St. Peter's) that outdid the Pantheon (fig. 23). And Dürer could bring the new esthetic north across the

*Fig. 23  Michelangelo, appointed architect of St. Peter's in 1546, designed the dome to outdo the ancient Pantheon. When finished, eighty years later, it soared above 450 feet and was the largest church in Christendom. With the colonnade Bernini built to frame it, the ensemble triumphantly surpasses the classical architecture that inspired it.*

Alps (fig. 24). For the practitioners of the Baroque during the following century (in opera no less than in painting, sculpture, and architecture), the paying of homage to the ancients was still as central an obligation as it had been to their Florentine predecessors. Art historians may distinguish successive stylistic phases—High Renaissance, Mannerism, Baroque, Classicism—but the inspiration of antiquity meant that all the artistic movements of the age shared common interests, themes, and practices. Nor were the arts alone. When Machiavelli cited the

*Fig. 24   In his self-portrait of 1498, Dürer shows the effect of a recent visit to Renaissance Venice on the more sober art of Germany. While there, enjoying the growing admiration given to artists, he wrote, "Here I am a gentleman, at home only a parasite." The finery in the painting seems an act of homage to that memory.*

Roman Republic as an ideal polity, he was merely one in a long line of Renaissance figures for whom the example of antiquity was by far the most important means of justifying belief, behavior, and argument.

⁓

Not only was intellectual and artistic life transformed during these centuries, but so too was the very basis of western European society and culture in the Middle Ages: religious routine and belief. The heart of this upheaval, the Reformation, and the feature that links it unequivocally to the Renaissance in general, was its determination to return to the past. Its very name reflects its origins in the effort to restore (not shape anew) the true doctrines of the Church.

The theologians who laid the foundations for the split that was to divide western Christendom—John Wycliffe in England and Jan Hus in Bohemia—had sought truth and virtue in antiquity with no less enthusiasm than their recent Italian predecessor, Petrarch. Their call for a return to the Bible and the Fathers of the Church reflected the same impulse: backward-looking reform. And the theme was still pursued, a century later, by the most potent reformer of all, Martin Luther.

The campaign begun by Luther and his successors (that is, those who formulated and accepted all the variants of Protestantism, including the doctrines of the radical sects) sought to re-create what they considered a pure biblical Christianity, cleansed of its medieval encrustations. As Luther put it in the heady days of the Reformation:

> O what a happy time have we now in regard to the purity of doctrine! But alas, we little esteem it. After the Fathers came the pope, and with him came mischievous traditions and human ordinances. Like a breaking cloud and a deluge, they overflowed the church and snared consciences through friars, masses, etc. Every day the pope brought new abominable errors into the church of Christ.

That the ambition to restore purity paralleled Petrarch's return to antiquity goes almost without saying. Too often, however, the Reformation is seen as a kind of antithesis to the Renaissance, and indeed as the beginning of a new era in European history. Although it is true that humanists and the advocates of religious reform pursued different agendas, their insistence on the authority of the distant past bound them together as the two sides of the Renaissance coin. The statement "Erasmus laid the egg that Luther hatched" may ascribe to humanism more influence than it deserves in the story of the Reformation, but it reflects a fundamental similarity that enables us to treat both movements as markers of Renaissance culture.

The Reformation, however, had far more dire consequences. Perhaps the saddest feature of this era in European history was the brutality of the religious wars that it spawned. If the persecution of Jews was a constant until taken to new depths of ghastliness in the twentieth century, the spectacle of Christians killing one another in huge numbers for the sake of faith was unique to the sixteenth and seventeenth centuries. The acceleration of this descent into the abyss by the growing destructiveness of warfare, and its intensification by ambitious nobles, princes, and governments, merely made more conspicuous this landmark of the age.

∽

Within the broader culture of the Renaissance, one dimension occupied a kind of overlapping middle ground between the bookish commitments of humanism and the world-encompassing beliefs of religion. The many strands of occult and supernatural inquiry and practice that we lump together under the name of magic—from the "cunning" woman waving a talisman that would help a customer find a missing ring to the scholar poring through the arcana of Hermes Trismegistus—were hardly new. Most of them had a lineage that went back to antiquity. But they achieved a pervasiveness and power in the fifteenth and sixteenth centuries that gave the culture as a whole a distinctive tinge.

Their most notorious manifestation was the campaign against witchcraft that swept through Europe for about a century and a half, beginning early in the 1500s (fig. 25). Nothing on this scale had ever been seen before, and it engulfed all ranks of society. But in many respects it was merely one sign of the deep-rooted assumption that the world functioned in ways that went beyond both reason and religious faith. Prophets had direct visions of the future. Wizards had access to elusive rules that governed nature and mankind, as did

*Fig. 25    Hans Baldung Grien's 1519 depiction of a Sabbath is an early indication of Europe's growing obsession with witches and their nefarious practices.*

astrologers, alchemists, and those who claimed to understand a literature of esoteric texts that derived its authority from the same confidence in antiquity that served Cicero or the Bible. Thus the impenetrable writings of Hermes Trismegistus, a figure from the beginnings of time whose "wisdom" was supposedly divinely inspired (though in fact written around the year 300, as a Renaissance scholar demonstrated), inspired awe partly because they were incomprehensible. Much the same was true of the most famous alchemist and magician of the six-teenth century, Paracelsus, who burned books he deplored but won admiration for arcane experiments and even more arcane writings that offered unfathomable insights into the mysteries of nature and life. Having one's horoscope cast was the equivalent, in the sixteenth or seventeenth centuries, of a visit to the psychiatrist in the twentieth. That such epitomes of rational thought as Robert Boyle and Isaac Newton should still have considered alchemy and biblical prophecy as forms of reasoned inquiry was but one symptom of the continuing quest for a sudden, comprehensive unlocking of the hidden mysteries of the universe.

∽

Like the Reformation, the Scientific Revolution is sometimes regarded as the antithesis of the Renaissance, a sure indicator that a new era had begun. There is no denying that, during the sixteenth and seventeenth centuries, a succession of probing philosophers, mathematicians, observers, and investigators re-defined the West's view of the natural world and the methods by which it should be explored. They turned natural philoso-phy into science. But to place them outside the era they inhab-ited is to give them a uniqueness they do not deserve.

For a start, the tradition of inquiry to which they belonged had venerable roots, having arisen in the wake of the revival of interest in Aristotle at the new universities of the late Middle Ages, notably Oxford and Padua. When academics discussed Nature at these institutions, they did so with Aristotle and other Greeks, such as Ptolemy and Galen, as their mentors. These ancients had originally posed the questions that were still being asked (for instance, why motion died out, as in an arrow's flight) and had also defined the methods—a combination of observation and reasoning—by which answers to those questions were still being sought. When Copernicus suggested a heliocentric model of the heavens, for example, he was careful to cite a precedent for his views from Greek philosophy. Well into the seventeenth century, the acknowledgment of this debt remained essential to the work of natural philosophers as they became "scientists."

Moreover, the unearthing and analysis of lost ancient texts was as important in this field of learning as in others. The most famous example is that of Archimedes, whose appearance in print in 1543 pushed the study of physics into new and fruitful directions. But even without such discoveries, the reliance on the past remained unmistakable. If, to Galileo and Descartes, Aristotle and Plato were still profound inspirations, that put them in the same camp as Petrarch and the religious reformers. All were engaged in enterprises that began by looking to antiquity for guidance. The natural philosophers might eventually have felt that they were moving beyond their mentors. Galileo, after all, gave the name of Simplicius, the most famous commentator on Aristotle, to the figure in his dialogue about astronomy who remains stuck in traditional geocentrism and has constantly to be shown the errors of his beliefs (fig. 26). Nevertheless, even Newton, in the next generation, pointed out the power of the ancients' insights into nature. Although his comment about pygmies standing on the shoulders of giants was intended to insult the physically disfigured Robert Hooke, it still reflected his profound reverence for the past.

⁓

*Fig. 26 The frontispiece of Galileo's* Dialogue on the Two Chief World Systems *(1632) shows the three figures whose conversation about astronomy in the book led to his trial by the Inquisition.*

One of the shaky clichés of Renaissance history is that this was when the world became secular, when religion was banished to a minor corner of the imagination. That Jacob Burckhardt labeled a central section of his masterly account of the period "The Discovery of the World and of Man" merely encouraged this view. As he noted, there arose an appreciation of nature for its own sake, and not only as a reflection of God's glory, that had far-reaching effects on philosophy and the arts. It was not insignificant that among Petrarch's most famous and unprecedented acts was his climbing of a mountain to see the view.

Once on top of the mountain, however, he reminded himself, with the help of St. Augustine (whom he revered), that one could not let such enjoyments divert one from the spiritual purposes of life. In other words, the discovery of the world was a strictly limited enterprise, completely overshadowed by the demands of faith. That truth has to be remembered as one traverses these centuries, particularly when one tries to come to terms with the extremes of religious passion that grew out of the Reformation. Nevertheless, there are a number of indications that a slow departure from traditional norms and explanatory systems was under way.

Avoiding both overstatement and understatement is not easy in this situation. One has to tread a fine line between drawing excessive implications from gradual shifts and dismissing their importance entirely. So long as one does not overplay their meaning, however, one can note the unmistakable signs of a diminishing reliance on the authority of faith or the divine. To the extent that, in several areas, the material world was coming to be judged and dealt with in its own terms, secularization was on its way.

One such area, central to the creativity of the age, was the fascination with the cultures of the ancient world. Much of this had to do with a quest for virtue, and was riddled with anxiety about the admiration for non-Christians. But much, also, reflected a hedonism and a love of beauty and elegance for their own sakes that hitherto had been carefully guarded. That this was a triumphant time for Ovid, and in particular for the sensuous tales of the *Metamorphoses,* speaks volumes about the predilections of the literate classes. No poet was more broadly read; none had so pervasive an influence on the arts. Although any story could be allegorized into a Christian message, the enthusiasm for Ovid and his themes revealed an earthiness that was very different from, say, the pious admiration for Virgil during the Middle Ages.

In the world of politics, the very expression of Machiavellian ideas, combined with the desacralization of kingship, revealed how openly the divine could now be separated from the exercise of authority. It was this drawing of lines that was the surest sign of a new outlook. When Galileo explained to the Grand Duchess of Tuscany that biblical arguments could not undermine the conclusions he had drawn from observation and mathematics, he was defining the same decisive divide. It was not that he (or Machiavelli) believed any less in the need for salvation or the essential place of the Church in his life. But he had separated the realms, and to the degree that there were limits on the role of faith, he had acknowledged the authenticity of the secular.

Equally revealing was how limited a role René Descartes ascribed to the divine in his *Discourse on Method* of 1637, the most influential work of philosophy of the seventeenth century. It is true that, after outlining the doubts about the possibility of truth that had assailed him, Descartes established a basis for certainty in his famous assertion that he knew he existed because he was thinking, and then immediately proved the existence of God. But the rest of the *Discourse* leaves theology aside. Remarkably, Descartes' faith-driven critic, Blaise Pascal, felt he had to make a case for the belief in God by applying his work on mathematical probability to the notion that it made more sense to wager on the existence of God than to bet against it. Philosophy was moving in directions that gave secular interests an ever-growing role.

The devout Catholic, Pascal, could justify religion by reference to science, but the acceptance of the worthiness of the secular realm was far more a product of Protestantism. The assertion that there is a priesthood of all believers, and that all vocations are equally worthy—two basic Protestant doctrines—gave life in this world, rather than the next, a stature that it had not previously had. The abandonment of the denunciation of usury, as capitalist behavior spread, had a similar effect. Again and again, one finds the supremacy of religious purposes and the dependence on theology undermined by the steadily increasing appeal of secular concerns. Nowhere was this more apparent than in education.

⤳⤶

Medieval universities were designed to produce clerics, lawyers, and doctors. They taught what had been defined in late antiquity as the seven branches of learning, or liberal arts, but they did so only with these professions in mind. And there were not many of these institutions: perhaps twenty, scattered across Europe, by 1300.

From the fourteenth century, however, there was an explosion in the founding of universities. By 1500 the number had risen to about one hundred, and over the next century or so (especially as competing Protestant and Catholic institutions were created) the total continued to grow. Moreover, they began to attract an entirely different clientele. The future professionals continued to come, and indeed developed a self-consciousness and forms of self-definition, organization, and self-regulation in this period that they had not had before. But newcomers also came in significant numbers: members of those very aristocratic families that were now coming to see themselves as superior in taste and refinement, not merely in valor. Their heirs and younger sons descended on the universities to acquire the veneer of education that increasingly was regarded as a mark of the elite. These newcomers were splendid sources of income for municipalities; thus, in their efforts to fund their university, which spread their fame throughout Europe, the ingenious Paduans even taxed local prostitutes. It was perhaps appropriate that, when the students who benefited from the tax were enraged by a rival college, they organized a nude protest. Universities, in other words, were taking on boisterous qualities that placed them ever more firmly within a secular world.

Above all, though, was their effect in changing the outlook of the elite. To some extent the new students were learning skills that might perhaps make them better managers of great estates. But far more important was the access they gained to a literary and philosophical milieu that previously had been of no interest to them.

A stint at London's Inns of Court, for example, though on the one hand essential for the professional training of lawyers, was also a nice finishing school for ambitious young men such as Walter Ralegh, who openly admitted that his time there had been merely a stepping stone to the life of a courtier. He later said that he never looked at a word of law while at the Inns. It had been a mechanism by which a young man coming from a distant county, Devon, could settle in London, near the royal court, and go about attracting attention as a wit, a poet, and a swordsman. When a country gentleman such as Ralegh sat in Parliament, moreover, and bandied about Latin phrases and quotations from ancient authors, he not only expected to be understood by his colleagues but also hoped to be admired.

The devotion to Latin could become obsessive and lifeless—one scholar's party trick was to give the next line for any given classical quotation, until one day he had to recite, as follow-up, the phrase *stultus ego,* "I'm a fool"—but it did help define the educated elite.

Accompanying this expansion of the university's role was a major overhaul of Europe's schools. This was to some extent the result of a widening recognition of childhood as a distinct stage of life, reflected in the portraits of individual children that became common in the sixteenth century. More specifically, however, it was a consequence of Petrarch's call for a return to the values of the ancient world. Although a large segment of primary and secondary education remained the province of the Church and religious orders, even there the growing influence of the call to emulate Rome was felt. The humanist schools founded in Italy by followers of Petrarch created a curriculum that required pupils to memorize the works of Latin authors, and that model was widely imitated. If they still had to struggle for centuries with the adherents of medieval scholasticism at schools and universities (a traditionalism that remained a major obstacle to new ideas, as Galileo found out), their focus on secular learning nevertheless had widespread effects. When sports became a part of school life; when the Jesuits founded, in 1557, a school for girls (the first of its kind) so as to teach them, too, the latest subjects; when classical literature and the new ideas of mathematics became staples of the most prized educational institutions; when the very concept of a profession burst its traditional bounds and could encompass, in a survey published in 1585, more than 150 career categories; and when a stay at university (not always for a degree) emerged as the mark of the educated man, there was no mistaking the increasingly secular concerns that accompanied the dramatic expansion of education during the Renaissance.

∾

One could add dozens of features that entered western society and culture in these years. This was when gypsies first appeared in Europe; when the study we know as Egyptology was conceived; when playing cards became popular; when ordinary people began to sit on chairs; when the shape of the indoor theater and a new art form for it to house, opera, were invented; when hallmarks came to be required for silver objects; when glass manufacture became cheaper, which allowed people of even modest means, for the first time in history, to insulate and close off small rooms and thus, as the Dutch artists Vermeer and de Hooch documented, to enjoy individual privacy; when the vehemence against the Middle Ages caused the great medieval philosopher Duns Scotus to become the source for a new word, "dunce"; when mechanical clocks became common features of urban life; when artists rose in social status from craftsmen to aristocrats, and their creativity came to be seen as a divine gift; when violent participatory sports became a regular form of recreation; when aristocratic women began to use parasols; and much else besides. But the major features outlined above are of sufficient range and magnitude to justify the view that this was indeed a distinct new era in history. We must now ask how and why it came to an end.

# Chapter Four

# CIVILIZATION IN CRISIS

*E*ven as Europeans created new forms of political and economic behavior, and new standards of intellectual and artistic creativity, to replace the eroding ideals of the Middle Ages, so they eventually set in motion the forces that would undermine the unities of the ensuing age, the Renaissance. What went wrong, when, and why?

To answer those questions, we must focus first on a span of just a few decades, about halfway through the three centuries that comprised the Renaissance, when tensions arose that eventually forced changes in priorities and outlook. The long-term effects of these changes were to drive Europe toward a new set of coherences, a new age.

The decisive period extended across a handful of decades around 1500, when a succession of crucial events unfolded that were logical outcomes of the new interests of the Renaissance, but ultimately proved destructive of its ideals. Emerging from the period's distinctive features (as outlined in the previous

chapter), they seemed to expand the possibilities that had unfolded over the previous century and a half. At the same time,
however, they caused tensions and uncertainties that would
take another century and a half to resolve. When, eventually,
the upheavals subsided—when their effects became an accepted part of the landscape—the result was the creation of a
new era in European civilization that one could no longer identify as the Renaissance.

⟨⟩

The basic transformation that came earliest on to the scene
was the least visible when it began, but it was to be no less potent than its more visible companions: a sharp rise in population, after more than a century of decline. At first, this growth
accelerated economic change and seemed purely beneficent,
but when the numbers again turned downward the effects
were to be serious.

Only in exceptional circumstances, such as the onset of the
Black Death, can one be fairly certain about the reasons that
large populations enter periods of decline or growth. The reasons for growth are especially difficult to determine, and the
shift from shrinkage or stagnation toward the increase that occurred in much of Europe during the second half of the fifteenth century is no exception. A gradual climatic warming,
causing better crop yields, is one possibility; another is a lowered level of virulence, or perhaps a drop in frequency, in the
regular visitations of plague. Both these hypotheses imply a re-
duction in rates of mortality; alternatively, there might have
been a rise in birth rates. Causes aside, however, there is broad
agreement that between roughly 1450 and 1600, Europe's population increased by about 50 percent, from some 50 million to

75 million. More important than the growth itself, however, were its effects.

To our eyes, the numbers involved seem trivial. But contemporaries eventually grew worried. Walking through the ever-more-crowded streets of London during the reign of Elizabeth I, Sir John Hawkins complained that England "is pestered now and choked through want of ground." So bad were things becoming for his fellow countrymen that "for the want of place they crawl one o'er another's back." This may sound like nonsense in view of the more than tenfold increase that was to come over the next four hundred years, but one should not minimize the sense of disruption. It was certainly true that towns—always the most crammed, diseased, and dangerous concentrations of people—were becoming more conspicuous, and this only reinforced the impression of overpopulation. It has been estimated that the proportion of those who lived in towns of more than 10,000 rose by about half between 1500 and 1650, reaching well above 10 percent of the total population in northwestern Europe and along the Mediterranean. There was a long way to go before one could speak of an urbanized continent, but this early leap was a major and significant step in that direction. Impressions of size are always relative, but it is telling that some, like Hawkins, found the sense of rapid change an unsettling challenge to assumptions about a traditional order.

Equally disturbing was one of the chief consequences of population growth: a rise in food prices that moved even faster in response to soaring demand. Between the late fifteenth century and 1600, in little more than a hundred years, the price of grain almost quadrupled. An annual rate of inflation of approximately 2 percent does not seem especially dramatic; but in an age when the notion of a "just price" for bread was taken for granted, the erosion of that belief was not lightly received, and by the seventeenth century the food riot was a common occurrence in much of Europe.

In the burgeoning cities, moreover, poverty was more distinct than in the countryside, where it was less concentrated and tended to blur into the background. As a result, beggars became more visible. In his autobiography, Thomas Platter, a Swiss printer of the sixteenth century, gave a vivid picture of the beggar's life he had endured in his early days; and the Flemish artist Peter Brueghel brought the crippled and the destitute of his day to life in his canvases (fig. 27). One was surrounded by constant reminders of the comment by Jesus in the Gospel of St. Mark: "Ye have the poor with you always."

With all that said, it was nevertheless clear that the "long" sixteenth century was essentially a boom age. Those who could produce surplus food; those who were involved in the building, mining, or armaments trades; and those who played their cards shrewdly as international trade quickened, shipbuilding expanded, and new markets opened overseas: All did well. Wages did lag behind prices—the classic consequence of population increase when the demand for goods rises, but labor becomes more available—and there were probably more losers than winners as landowners raised rents, enclosed fields for pasture, and encouraged the "putting-out" system. Nevertheless, one can hardly conclude that the economic advances of the century— fueled by population growth, perhaps, but also by broadening capitalist impulses—were moving Europe toward societal breakdown. After all, England and the Netherlands witnessed the first steps toward what was to be an "agricultural revolution" in the eighteenth century when, for the first time in history, a rise in crop yields matched the growth in the number of

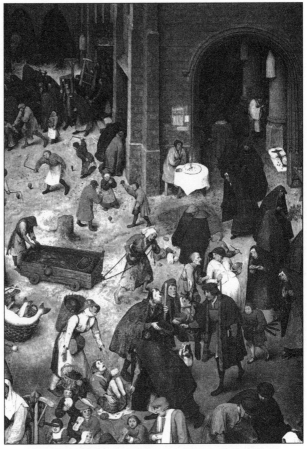

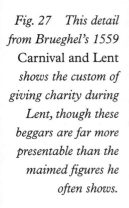

*Fig. 27 This detail from Brueghel's 1559* Carnival and Lent *shows the custom of giving charity during Lent, though these beggars are far more presentable than the maimed figures he often shows.*

people. Land reclamation, new crops and fertilizers, and experimental planting techniques were soon to give farmers the capacity to support enormous growth in the number of Europeans.

For the origins of a growing sense of crisis, we have to look, not at this expansion, but at the effects when, for a while, it ended: the demographic and economic reverses that brought the boom to an end in the second quarter of the seventeenth century. The crucial downturn was widely signaled by the 1620s. The number of ships passing the Sound, the entrance to the Baltic, fell dramatically in that decade. At the same time, the imports of silver from the New World began to spiral downwards. For both north and south Europe these were ominous indicators, reinforced by a slump in textile production, a mainstay of traditionally prosperous areas such as northern Italy, Flanders, England, and northern France. When James I summoned England's Parliament in 1621, he "commended one thing of singular importance . . . , which was the cause of the want and decay of money," and the members outdid one another in citing evidence of hardship and poverty. With the study of economic behavior still in its infancy, blame was showered in all directions, but it now seems that the most likely culprit was a severe trade crisis in 1619–1621, when currency manipulations, shortage of supply, and the disruptions of the Thirty Years' War triggered a reversal in more than a century of growth.

It is true that northwestern Europe, especially the Dutch and the English, weathered the storm more comfortably than the rest of Europe. (By 1700 this was the one area that had not only recovered the population levels of 1600 but had exceeded them significantly.) But everywhere else this was a century of struggle, probably exacerbated by a period of maximum climatic cooling starting around 1650 that is associated with a "little ice age." In particular, two of the leading economic powers of previous generations, Venice and Spain, suffered slumps so severe that they never again enjoyed a dominant role in international trade. The center of gravity shifted definitively from the Mediterranean, where it had remained for millennia, to northern Europe.

There is no straight path from economic difficulties to other forms of unrest, but it is hard not to believe that the successive disruptions of economic life—first the unexpected boom after more than a century of depression, and then, even more troubling, a sharp rebuff to the steadily rising expectations of the sixteenth century—were without effect. One of the major blows to the coherence of medieval society had been the demographic and economic collapse of the fourteenth century. This one was nowhere near as dramatic, but it must be seen as essential background to the other deteriorations that prompted a sense of crisis in the mid-seventeenth century. And one of the offshoots of economic and demographic change, the movement of Europeans overseas, was to have its own disturbing implications.

⁕

One date above all has etched the decades close to 1500 into the consciousness of the West: 1492. Christopher Columbus's voyage was the starting point for a transformation in global history, not merely the history of Europe. Yet its place in the Renaissance has to be seen in the context of an outward reach that not only had medieval antecedents—in the colonization of eastern Europe and the Crusade expeditions to the Middle East—but also a more immediate origin in the expansion of Portugal during the fifteenth century. The latter movement, as sailors, navigators, geographers, and astronomers probed the African coastline and eventually found the sea route to India, was one of the most remarkable achievements of Renaissance Europe. The leaders of this tiny country, hoping to promote new sources of wealth and the advance of Christianity, were almost ideal exemplars of the adventurousness, the curiosity, and the hard-nosed pragmatism that were so characteristic of the age.

When other rulers, envious of Portugal's success, joined the quest for discovery overseas, their motivations were little different. And the 1490s proved to be the decade of their most spectacular breakthroughs, not only by Columbus, who headed west, but also by Vasco da Gama, who sailed round Africa and reached India for the Portuguese. From this point on, the Europeans never looked back; by 1700, approximately 1 million of them were living overseas. The relentless march of their fleets, their soldiers, their missionaries, and their settlers swept through the Americas and the coasts of Africa and southern Asia. No other element of the economic growth of these years did as much to change the face of Europe. Yet the expansion of the overseas empires, connected as it was to the quickening pace of economic life in general, must also be related to the mid-seventeenth-century sense of crisis. As we have already seen, the downturn in both population and economy after 1600 was an essential background to that crisis. But the exploration of new lands, too, was a source of disquiet and unease.

That unknown lands existed at all was troubling enough. Why had nobody heard about them before? Even more disturbing: What about their inhabitants? How was it possible that they, too, had descended from Adam and Eve (fig. 28)?

Moreover, as the French writer Michel de Montaigne soon noted, their behavior cast doubt on truths that Europeans had long taken for granted. Following a long conversation with a cannibal who had been brought to France, Montaigne used the encounter to reprimand his countrymen:

*Fig. 28 When John White's drawing of an Indian village in the 1580s was engraved, it gave a visual underpinning to the European image of a very different New World.*

I find that there is nothing barbarous or savage in this nation, except that we call barbarism whatever we ourselves do not do. Indeed, we seem to have no definition of truth and reason other than the opinions and customs of the place where we live. These people are wild in the same sense that we say fruits, produced by nature alone, are wild.

I do not regret mentioning the barbaric horror of the cruelty [of their cannibalism], but I am sorry that, even as we condemn their faults, we are so blind to our own. I think it more barbaric to eat a man alive than dead; it is worse to tear a body apart on the rack while it still has feeling, or to burn a man alive, than to roast and eat him after he is dead.

Montaigne, skeptical at all times, could not bring himself to insist unequivocally on the lessons he had learned from his encounter. Questioning the significance of his conversation at the end of his essay, he mentions, without further ado, that cannibals don't even wear trousers—a typically ambiguous comment that might reflect on European dress codes as much as on the shortcomings of cannibal wisdom.

Yet the doubts that were raised about European morals by the people whom the explorers met were not merely a matter of relative values. Far more alarming, at least to some observers, was the depravity that conquest itself exposed. The most notable of the critics, the Spanish friar Bartolomé de las Casas, was scathing as he described the viciousness of his fellow-Spaniards:

God made all the peoples of [the New World], many and varied as they are, as open and as innocent as can be imagined. It was upon these gentle lambs that from the very first day they clapped eyes on them the Spanish fell like ravening wolves upon the fold, or like tigers and savage lions who have not eaten meat for days. The pattern established at the outset has remained unchanged to this day, and the Spaniards still do nothing save tear the natives to shreds, murder them and inflict upon them untold misery, suffering and distress, tormenting, harrying and persecuting them mercilessly.

These voices were exceptional, but they were widely heard. And although the views of Montaigne and Las Casas had no noticeable effect on their contemporaries, the challenge they offered to comfortable assumptions was profound and far-reaching.

It was not only in the realm of ideas that the overseas empires prompted doubts. The silver, spices, and other commodities that flowed into Europe as a result of the discoveries certainly created great wealth. But we have seen that rapid economic change could be a two-edged sword. Moreover, the hardships of the travelers and settlers were a constant theme: Many more died trying to colonize Virginia, for example, than remained alive at the end of its first twenty years. The doubts about such enterprises, and the financial losses they often caused, served as a depressing drumbeat alongside the trumpetings of newfound wealth and patriotic glory. "We must have gold before we see England," insisted Sir Francis Drake as his final voyage floundered in disaster. The refusal to admit failure amidst so many opportunities for triumph proved fatal to him and to tens of thousands of other seamen and settlers.

It was bad enough that the exploitation of natives and slaves raised unhappy questions about Christian behavior. It was worse that the expansion brought adversity in doses often equal to fortune. Worst of all, the overseas rivalries exacerbated the rising violence of an increasingly war-torn age. Ambitious and aggressive rulers hardly needed additional stimuli for their belligerence, but they found them in the competition for empire. The Spanish, Dutch, and English, for instance, had plenty of reasons to fight one another, but it is clear that events overseas multiplied their animosities.

The various doubts that the discoveries prompted did not as yet loom large, but they were one more disturbing presence as Europeans struggled to come to terms with the consequences of the transformations that had begun around 1500. And none of these had a more pervasive impact than the revolution in the conduct of war.

∞

Although gunpowder's possibilities had been known for some time, its transformation of armed conflict did not take hold until late in the fifteenth century. Some cannon had appeared earlier on the battlefield and at sieges, and the first steps had been taken toward the production of hand guns, but the so-called Hundred Years' War between the English and the French (ending in the 1450s), and the later struggle between the kings of France and the dukes of Burgundy, were still decided largely by traditional means: mounted armored knights, pikemen, archers, and infantry carrying a variety of lethal but not fire-launched weapons. Not until the Italian wars, which pitted the Habsburg dynasty of Spain and the Empire against the Valois dynasty of France, and continued intermittently from the 1490s to the 1550s, was it clear that gunpowder had become a decisive military tool.

Having been proved essential, the new technology began to shape consequences, during the next century, that went far beyond the battlefield. We have already seen the effect it had on the self-image of the aristocrat, and we will soon see how it accelerated changes in politics, in the power of governments, and in diplomatic affairs. But the most corrosive effect came from the very conduct of the military. The sheer destructiveness of the new weapons raised fears, as conflict became widespread during the Thirty Years' War, especially when the war expanded in the 1630s, that Europe was approaching an abyss of uncontrollable mayhem. These were parlous times—in the words of a preacher speaking in England's Parliament in the 1640s, "These are days of shaking, . . . and this shaking is universal." To many, it seemed conceivable that the mayhem might make the restoration of stability impossible.

The ever-larger armies—there might have been some 300,000 men under arms in the battlegrounds of the 1630s and 1640s, not to mention the hundreds of thousands more who were needed to keep the soldiers in the field—brought famine and disease in their wake. They created a sense of dread and crisis more intense than any of the other disruptive forces of the age. Moreover, the outlays required to raise and equip a gunpowder army meant that princes gained a monopoly on the use of force at the very time that those armies' capacity for destruction and intimidation increased geometrically. The power that was now available was irresistible, but only a government, empowered by taxation, could afford the soaring costs that the new firearms and the multiplying troops demanded. And only a government could assemble the bureaucracy that was needed to raise the taxes and organize the troops. The chicken-and-egg argument about whether military needs led to the strengthening of the state or vice versa might never be resolved; but that the two joined together to transform politics as well as war, and to force Europeans to struggle with a brave new world, is beyond question.

It was again in the decades close to 1500 that a group of determined rulers, appropriately known to history as "new monarchs," began to seek expanded powers over their subjects, and in so doing set in motion long-term political consequences that have come to be summed up as state-building or state formation. If the grandiose outcomes of their policies could not have been foreseen at this stage, that is equally true of the demographic shift, the rise of gunpowder, and all the other transforming influences of the age, including even the most immediately disruptive of them all, the Reformation. That the leading players of these decades had no idea they were beginning to move their civilization in new directions in no way lessens the importance of their actions and policies.

This is especially true of the "new monarchs" who ruled Spain, France, and England in the late 1400s and early 1500s. They may have had only limited success in consolidating their territories and imposing their authority on their subjects, especially by comparison with the accomplishments of their descendants. And it is undeniable that, for the most redoubtable prince of the first half of the sixteenth century, Emperor Charles V, the kingdom of Spain was but one of many realms. His driving inspiration was the ancient ideal of imperial glory created by Augustus and his Roman successors, not a well-organized and aggressive single realm. Nor is there any evidence that these princes were self-consciously expanding royal powers or fashioning new structures of government. They all saw themselves as addressing immediate though long-standing problems, and relying on centuries of established procedure and behavior in everything they did. Yet the very energy with which they pursued their aims gave political change in their realms a momentum that was to prove irresistible.

It does not lessen that conclusion to identify the chief and constant purpose of Ferdinand and Isabella in Spain, of Louis XI and his successors in France, and of the early Tudors in England as their determination to keep their crowns from being overwhelmed by the aristocrats and grandees among whom they often seemed merely the first among equals. One of the great stories of the age concerns the bone-crunching three-day ride Isabella of Castile took to the city of Leon to make sure she would be able to take command of the powerful knightly order of Santiago. The queen was willing to keep going through the night because the rule of the order stated that, if the monarch was present at the election, held just a few days after the death of the previous master, she could claim the post for herself. A vital opportunity such as this, to gain control of one of the major organizations of aristocratic (and hence military) power in her kingdom, could not be missed.

The reigns of the Spanish, French, and English monarchs in these years were filled with such episodes. Again and again, shrewd, forceful, and ambitious rulers took crucial steps to consolidate royal authority. In Spain, they mastered the great chivalric orders; they developed a tax system that provided a steady flow of revenue for the crown; they created a large standing army; they completed a centuries-long crusade with the capture of the last Moorish territory in Europe, the kingdom of Granada; they Christianized Spain with the expulsion of Jews and Moors; they asserted Spanish power abroad, first in Italy and then in the New World, which proved to be the source of immense new wealth; and finally, in the reign of Charles V (Charles I to Spaniards), they began the early elaboration of a legal and bureaucratic system without equal in its reach throughout society. As political power became ever more centralized (a process symbolized by the creation of a new capital, Madrid, at the geographic center of Castile), however, all the other regions of the realm became increasingly subordinated to Castile. In the rising tensions between provinces and center—most starkly embodied in the revolt of the Spanish provinces in the Netherlands, where repression and resistance were memorably recorded by Brueghel (plate 5)—there lay the seeds of the major test state-building soon had to face.

If the Spaniards at first went faster and farther as they focused authority and built up the institutions of the state—at the expense of the traditional autonomy of the locality and the region—the French were not far behind. Here, too, the kings had to subdue major rivals, especially great nobles and princes who dominated areas far from Paris, and powerful churchmen. By the 1550s they had won notable victories in this struggle. Indeed, had their consolidation of authority—signaled by their expansion of tax revenues, the army, and the bureaucracy—not been interrupted by a devastating civil war that started in the early 1560s and continued for more than thirty years, France's monarchs might well have been able to mount a serious challenge to the Habsburgs and claim the political leadership of Europe long before they actually did so, in the mid-seventeenth century. As it was, the end of the civil wars marked the beginning of no less dramatic an effort of state-building. Here, as in Spain, bureaucrats proliferated, armed forces grew, and Paris sought to subdue all forms of local independence. As in Spain, too, the losers were to fight back.

Unlike Spain or France, sixteenth-century England did not develop a standing army or a large, intrusive bureaucracy, but in other ways the process of state-building was no less evident. Thus, when the first Tudor, Henry VII, came to the throne in

1485, he encountered the same problem of over-mighty sub-jects as his Continental counterparts. Faced with the task of re-building royal authority after thirty years of civil war, the Wars of the Roses, he restored his treasury and subdued rivals to such good effect that his son and his granddaughter, Henry VIII and Elizabeth I, could create one of the smoothest-running regimes in Europe. Instead of dispatching teams of royal servants, they relied on local cooperation to implement policy, a system that, at the highest levels, fostered the broad in-teraction between ruler and ruled that took place in Parliament. The reliance on this consultative and legislative body, however, ultimately caused difficulties for the government that were no less severe than those that challenged the kings of Spain and France. For all three, the assertion of royal power in the age of the "new monarchs" turned out to be the first stirrings of a process of state-building that ultimately, in the mid-seventeenth century, generated tensions that threw Europe's political rela-tions into crisis.

What began in the three western kingdoms had its reper-cussions elsewhere. It was largely in response to the invasion of his beloved Italy by the French and the Spaniards that Machi-avelli wrote his *Prince* in 1513—another landmark of these decades. Taking Ferdinand of Aragon as one of his models, Machiavelli laid out a vision of a secular politics that had not been seen since ancient Rome. His ideal might have been a Ci-ceronian republic, but the quest for control that he described captured the essence of the assertive princes of his day. And his analysis of their behavior was one of the foundations for the rising interest among political theorists in the nature of sover-eignty and in the ways governments could justify the exercise of power over their subjects.

As the notion of a territorially defined centralized state began to crystallize, it combined with the growing expense and destructiveness of war to exacerbate tensions, not only between governments and subjects but also among states. That this no longer meant just the relations among individual princes was becoming clear from the development, within a century or so after Machiavelli, of a body of literature that sought to define international law. The Spaniard Francisco Suarez and the Dutchman Hugo Grotius came to suggest that, in addition to divine will, there was a system of "natural" law that made it possible to judge the behavior of states as well as individuals. Such ideas became especially relevant when the chaos of the Thirty Years' War intensified in the 1620s and 1630s, and it became clear that traditional forms of peacemaking between princes were incapable of countering the growing anarchy of international relations. Hitherto, a small group of protagonists—often just two or three—would sign an accord to bring a dispute to an end. Now the marauding armies that roamed across Germany and central Europe seemed completely out of control, certainly beyond the power of just a few combatants to subdue. A sense of doom, of irresolvable crisis, began to echo through the writings of the time, and only an entirely new approach to peacemaking, based on the concept of an international system governed by law, was able to resolve the crisis.

The result, the remarkable five-year effort of steady negotiation among 109 official delegations, representing nearly 200 interested parties, in the northwestern German province of Westphalia, which culminated in the peace treaties of 1648, was a landmark in the history of diplomacy. Never before had it been thought possible, in essence, to redraw the map of Europe. And this was accomplished despite the divide between

Protestants (who met in Münster) and Catholics (who met in Osnabrück, half a day's ride away). It was a measure of how seriously the chaos of the Thirty Years' War was regarded that so many of Europe's leaders were willing to give so much time to produce a settlement. Despite the endless obstacles, including the sense that the war itself was out of control, they persevered. Simply by remaining together for so long (though ambassadors did shuttle in and out, each departure and arrival serving as the occasion for splendid parties), poring over newly drawn maps, and working out procedures for themselves, the participants basically created the diplomatic system and the standard for international agreements that were to dominate Europe for centuries to come (fig. 29). It is true that, despite having an astute representative at the discussions—Cardinal Chigi, a member of a great family of Sienese bankers and himself a future pope—the papacy saw fit to denounce the final treaties as inimical to the interests of the Church. But the anathema was ignored, even by Catholics: a sign not only of the relief that the war's ravages had been ended but also of the waning influence of confessional hatreds.

Above all, the Westphalia peace treaties were noteworthy because they signaled a recognition throughout Europe that the political developments of the previous century and a half had plunged the continent into a crisis of massive proportions that required unprecedented action to resolve. If Westphalia was the first success in that endeavor—and in some ways the first sign that the extent of the crisis had been acknowledged by contemporaries—it was soon to be followed by others.

The 1640s in fact proved to be not merely a low point in international relations (it is telling that, despite the peace treaties, it proved impossible to bring the violence of the warring armies

*Fig. 29   Gerard Terborch shows himself (on the far left, looking at the viewer) amongst the Dutch and Spanish diplomats who ratified their part of the Peace of Westphalia in 1648. The man with his hand on the Bible is the Spanish nobleman whom Terborch (though a Dutchman) was serving at the time.*

to an end for another five years) but also a moment of acute instability *within* states. During this decade the mounting resentments caused by the growth of central governments finally burst into open resistance. From the revolution led by Cromwell in England to the revolts faced by the kings of Spain and France, and the upheavals in places as far flung as Holland, Sweden, East Prussia, Naples, and Portugal, the 1640s and 1650s became a time when subjects fought their rulers on a scale that had never before been seen in European history, and was not to recur until the 1790s. The trampling of local and regional rights by assertive central governments had created a multitude of flash points no less dangerous than those that the same assertiveness had sparked in international relations. Here, as in the worlds of religion and thought, the invention of printing had a corrosive effect. Not only did it spawn a new phenomenon, the newspaper, which could distribute subversive criticisms of established authority, but it also made available discussions of the nature of government, the so-called *arcana imperii,* which undermined the monopoly of rulers over the secrets of their trade. The newspaper was made especially dangerous by its link to a new gathering place, the offspring of a product new to Europe: coffee. The coffee shop was a rapidly proliferating seventeenth-century invention, almost always stocked with newspapers. By the 1680s, the scene was becoming a staple of Restoration Comedy, its denizens' conversation summed up in the verse "It must be true, for I read it in the papers, didn't you?" Here were the first stirrings of the creation of an unprecedented kind of public space and public discourse—what has been called a new "public sphere," which eventually had powerful political effects that transformed social relations beyond repair.

For princes and their counselors, just as for merchants, explorers, and warriors, therefore, the crisis of the mid-seventeenth century demanded a rethinking of the ways they dealt with the world. The economic, military, and political developments we have seen to be characteristic of the Renaissance were bursting at the seams. To restore stability, Europe would have to move beyond them and enter a new era.

⚬⚮⚬

Of all the events that gave the decades from 1490 to 1520 their world-historical importance none (not even Columbus's voyages across the Atlantic) was as dramatic as Luther's protest against the Church. As in the other developments of the time, moreover, it was by no means clear at first that a German monk's criticism of current ecclesiastical practices, especially the Church's money-raising devices, would have such far-reaching effects, though there was no denying that the new medium of print made his ideas widely accessible. Even when Luther decided to break with the papacy, however, and argued that priestly authority and a reliance on rituals were unnecessary for salvation, few would have predicted that he could split western Christendom apart. But the alternative he proposed, salvation by faith and the words of Scripture alone, caught fire, and soon Rome felt compelled to launch a counteroffensive to regain its lost souls.

The Reformation that began when Luther launched his campaign in 1517 was a quintessential Renaissance movement: It was spawned by dissatisfaction with medieval institutions as they lost their authority in the fourteenth century and by the reverence for the distant past that was characteristic of the new age. But the effects of this quest for spiritual renewal were devastating. Less than twenty years after Luther's initial challenge to Church doctrine there began the first of a series of religious wars that continued for approximately a century. If there was a central cause for the growing sense of crisis in European civilization during these years, it was the gradual realization that western Christendom, once united and coherent, was falling into irreparable disarray.

Every major conflict that broke out from the 1530s to the 1640s—and there were dozens—was exacerbated by religious passions. Other forces might have been at work, from territorial

*Fig. 30   François Dubois painted this symbolic depiction of the violence of the St. Bartholomew's Day Massacre in Paris and much of France in 1572. The disposal of the corpses in a river, to cleanse the city of heresy, accords with what we know of the religious fury of the time.*

disputes to princely ambitions, but the intensity was primarily a product of faith. This was the source of the contempt, the determination to destroy, that marked the wars of this period as the most vicious and bloody that Europe experienced until the twentieth century. The Thirty Years' War, in particular, came to be regarded as the nadir of indiscriminate slaughter and brutality until it was trumped by World Wars I and II. But the other wars of religion were hardly more gentle. The belief that heresy polluted the earth, that (for instance) one could cleanse a community only by throwing the corpses of one's enemies into a body of water, was a feature of the civil wars that wracked France from the 1560s to the 1580s (fig. 30). Similar disdain animated Spaniards, Englishmen, Dutchmen, and others in these years.

One byproduct of the fear of heresy and the instinct to persecute deviancy was the witchcraft hysteria of the age. Among the many assaults on human dignity and decency, this was in some ways the most cruel. In an age when natural events such as the sudden death of a cow or the appearance of a skin rash lacked rational explanation, it was easy to fix the blame on an unpopular member of the community. The targets were often elderly women; indeed, their loneliness, poverty, and descent into the unconscious habits of old age, such as mumbling to themselves, made them inevitable victims. That they might previously have been regarded as repositories of wisdom did not prevent them from being accused, in difficult times, of having become consorts of the devil and founts of malevolence.

Europe's witch hysteria reached its most fervid extremes during the period when Protestants and Catholics alike showed utter disregard for human life. Witch-hunting was thus a symptom and an appropriate symbol for a culture in crisis. The quest for scapegoats, which was related to the escapism that drew people to prophets, messiahs, and magic, revealed the growing distress caused by the wars of religion. Calls for tolerance seemed to go unheeded, and political measures to reduce the anarchy—notably the Peace of Augsburg in Germany and the Edict of Nantes in France, both of which were attempts to impose toleration by law—seemed to have only limited effect. It was clear that religious commitment without compromise was the order of the day. If the violent effects of such an outlook were to be mitigated, a fundamental shift in belief and behavior would be necessary. That shift was to be essential to the resolution of the crisis, but it was also to mark the end of assumptions central to Renaissance Europe.

⤙

We have seen that, in one crucial arena, theology, the return to antiquity that was characteristic of the Renaissance had disturbing consequences. The rift in Christendom that began with Luther's attempt to return to the Bible and the early Fathers was to cause immense disquiet. And the invention of printing ensured not only a wide audience for the new ideas but an acceleration of their impact. Not surprisingly, one response to the upheavals that ensued was a return to another strain in ancient thought, skepticism. With antagonists asserting exclusive and incompatible versions of truth, it seemed only appropriate to question the very nature of such claims. As a result, the sixteenth century proved to be a golden age for the skeptic. From Erasmus's *Praise of Folly* on the eve of the Reformation through the powerful explorations of Montaigne, and on to Shakespeare's jesters and Cervantes' *Don Quixote,* the doubter and the seeming fool became beacons of wisdom. One writer became known as Sanchez the Skeptic; another published an entire book consisting solely of question marks.

Not unrelated was the revival of Stoic philosophy. Associated primarily with the work of Justus Lipsius of the Netherlands, this tradition was again intended as a defense against the uncertainty of the times. Lipsius's most famous work, *On Constancy* (1584), which derived its title from a similar work by the Roman philosopher Seneca, was a call for the kind of steadiness and self-discipline that was in short supply amidst the vicissitudes and fanaticism of religious war. Like skepticism, this down-to-earth belief in a practical, orderly, and moderate posture reflected the need to find a workable response to the demands of a changing world. The perceptive sociologist Norbert Elias argued that this effort to control the emotions should also be linked to the process of state-building because it clearly fostered the creation and maintenance of stable, impersonal structures. It is worth noting in this regard that one of the great admirers of Lipsius was the highly disciplined and impassive master of bureaucracy, Spain's Philip II. His calm demeanor as he struggled with terrible pain on his deathbed caused the Venetian ambassador, who watched the drama, to say that Philip had died so well it was as if he had practiced it before.

In the view of one distinguished student of this period, William Bouwsma, the rising importance of skepticism and Stoicism was a telling symptom of what he called the Waning of the Renaissance. It is hard to disagree with him. As he pointed out, the leading exemplars of the thinking of the late sixteenth and early seventeenth centuries—Jean Bodin and Michel de Montaigne in France; Richard Hooker, Francis Bacon, and Robert Burton in England; and Miguel de Cervantes, Justus Lipsius, and Paolo Sarpi in Spain, the Netherlands, and Italy—were riddled through with inconsistency, reversal, and often self-doubt. As Montaigne put it in a famous statement, "I may contradict myself, but I always speak the truth." Faced with the rival claims to truth of the religious combatants of the day, not to mention the disturbing implications of overseas discoveries and economic and political change, it was no wonder that indeterminacy and a moderate pragmatism seemed so appealing.

Skepticism and Stoicism, for all their reflections of disturbing times, could at least be justified in Renaissance terms by their distinguished lineage from antiquity. But one threat to received wisdom rejected the comfort of pedigree and raised a challenge not only to the great figures of the past but to the very reliance on their example that had animated Renaissance culture. This ultimately transformative strand of intellectual inquiry came from the investigation of natural philosophy.

～

Unknown until much later was one of the most pregnant breakthroughs of the 1490–1520 period: Nicolaus Copernicus's conclusion that the sun was the center of the solar system. His findings were not published until he lay on his deathbed in 1543, the same year that revolutions also began in the fields of anatomy (the publication of Vesalius's work on the human body) and physics (the rediscovery of Archimedes). As was typical of the age, these new directions remained rooted in, and justified by, the wisdom of antiquity. Copernicus explained his willingness to go against centuries of assumptions about the centrality of the earth by citing as precedent an array of Greek astronomers. Vesalius referred to the Hellenistic anatomist Galen, and Archimedes (long lost to western thought) was himself Greek.

One of the impulses behind these new explorations of nature was also a product of the obsession with antiquity. For Petrarch and many of his successors, the Roman world set the standard they sought to follow. But they were aware, especially through contacts with Byzantine scholars, that ancient Greece, too, offered models to be emulated. Aristotle was already well known, but not so his teacher, Plato. As mastery of Greek developed in the late fifteenth century—once again helped along by the patronage of the Medici—so did a new movement of revival, Neoplatonism. It has been argued that Copernicus's veneration of the sun derived from Platonic ideas, and certainly the very quest for simpler, all-embracing truths drew strength from Neoplatonic views.

For all their conservatism, however, the rethinkings of astronomy, anatomy, and physics that ensued proved to be foretastes of a fundamental change in the understanding of the natural world. That was especially so because of the focus on experimentation that also arose at this time—first from practitioners of alchemy and inveterate explorers of physical reality such as Paracelsus, and then from advocates of experiment such as Francis Bacon. What is important for our purposes, though, is not the eventual triumph of these ideas but how disconcerting they seemed for more than a century. The decades following the events of 1543 were a time of troubled uncertainty about the new ideas. Instead of sweeping all before them, the challenges to long-standing assumptions about the heavens, about the body, and about the principles of motion merely intensified the antagonisms, doubts, and confusions characteristic of the age. Not until the late seventeenth century did it become clear that the picture of the world that had been accepted since antiquity—the theories of Aristotle, Ptolemy, Galen, and their successors—had been overturned. In the meantime, the struggle between old and new seemed to leave confidence and truth beyond reach.

Montaigne included the speculations of Copernicus among the reasons for his skepticism. If an old idea had to give way to a new one, when would the process end, and how did one know where truth lay? When Kepler urged Galileo to publish, he did so in language that reflected the fraught circumstances of his time: "You advise us to retreat . . . and not to expose ourselves to the violent attacks of the mob of scholars. But . . . would it

*Plate 1    Masaccio's* Adam and Eve, *painted for the Brancacci Chapel in S. Maria del Carmine in Florence in the 1420s, is one of the first masterpieces created under the inspiration of ancient art. The three-dimensional figures, the Roman archway, and, above all, the anguish of the duo expelled from paradise exemplify the new interests of the Renaissance.*

*Plate 2   Botticelli's* Birth of Venus, *of 1486, is among the first quintessentially Renaissance paintings in that it presents a classical scene as a painter from antiquity might have shown it.*

*Plate 3    Cast in the 1480s, and placed in one of the city's main open spaces, Verrocchio's statue of the commander of Venice's troops, Bartolommeo Colleoni, captures the traditional view of the military hero, in full armor and on a splendid horse, as the embodiment of valor.*

*Plate 4    Titian's 1548 equestrian portrait of Charles V shows him
in the quintessential pose of a Renaissance prince as the victor of the
Battle of Mühlberg (1547). Echoing a famous sculpture of the Roman
emperor Marcus Aurelius, it emphasizes the heroism (and thus the
nobility) of the ruler as Christian knight, a warrior in full armor
riding a splendid horse.*

*Plate 5 Brueghel in 1565 resorted to a biblical story, the Massacre of the Innocents, to comment on the Spanish soldiers who were persecuting his Flemish countrymen during the early days of resistance to the rule of Spain.*

*Plate 6   Painted in 1629/1630, Rubens's* **Peace and War** *hints at a shift in his view of warfare. Mars looks in amazement at the pleasures and fertility of peace as a Fury draws him on, and Minerva, goddess of wisdom, stops him from spoiling the contentment he sees.*

*Plate 7    As with the Emperor Charles V, so with England's Charles I. He appears both as a warrior (fig. 16) and as a man of peace (compare fig. 15). Van Dyck's most famous portrait, from 1635, shows the king dressed as an elegant gentleman posing against a lovely landscape. In his hand is a walking stick instead of a commander's baton, and nearby his horse is being tended by a groom.*

*Plate 8    Watteau's Embarkation for Cythera (1717) exhibits the more relaxed atmosphere that artists embraced as the strivings of the Renaissance came to an end. His subjects are often elegant aristocrats engaged in pleasurable pursuits. Here, in soft tones, with cherubs flying above, they depart for the Greek isle of Cythera, famous for its cult of the goddess Aphrodite, to enjoy her gift of love.*

not be much better, . . . with powerful voices, to shout down the common herd?" Francis Bacon used an even more explicitly military analogy: "Nor is mine a trumpet which summons and excites men to cut each other to pieces, . . . but rather to make peace between themselves, and turning with armed forces against the Nature of Things, to storm and occupy her castles and strongholds, and extend the bounds of human empire." To outsiders, the ambitions of the scientists seemed almost comical. A Roman monsignor, for instance, on hearing that Galileo's astronomical ideas had run into trouble with the Church, wrote to a friend:

> The disputes of Signor Galileo have dissolved into alchemical smoke, since the Holy Office has declared that to maintain this opinion is to dissent manifestly from the infallible dogmas of the Church. So here we are at last, safely back on a solid Earth, and we do not have to fly with it as so many ants crawling around a balloon.

As late as 1637, René Descartes described his procedures as driven by uncertainty: "Like a man who walks alone in the darkness, I resolved to go so slowly and circumspectly that if I did not get ahead very rapidly I was at least safe from falling."

These were hardly the sentiments of pioneers sweeping all before them. The conquest was slow and tortuous; and, during the period when so much else in society seemed to undermine stability and assurance, the natural philosophers only made things worse. Who was right? How could one know? Questions like these eventually brought the pillars of Renaissance culture crashing down.

⚮

Two responses to the widening confusion of the age seemed at first to offer a means of reasserting a sense of control and order. Neither, however, was to offer a long-term answer to the crisis of the age.

First was the antiquarian impulse. One product of the humanist agenda to dig up as much as possible about antiquity was the development of a series of new disciplines, such as Egyptology, palaeography, epigraphy, and numismatics. As objects and oddities (often thought of as wonders) that previously had been ignored now came to be studied and desired, the fascination with the material world took new forms. Most remarkable was the so-called Cabinet of Curiosities, a collection of unusual items, ranging from a tiger's tooth to an ancient coin, that was assembled by a wealthy patron (fig. 31). The range was almost limitless, and could encompass gems and precious metals as well as the powder ground from a unicorn's horn (fig. 32).

The point, however, was to assemble a microcosm of the natural world in one place. If the collector assumed that the objects had magical properties, all the better, and it is significant that perhaps the most famous of these Cabinets—the one belonging to Emperor Rudolf II in Prague in the early seventeenth century—was put together by one of the period's most famous supporters of astrology, alchemy, and other magical arts.

A similar impulse led to the creation of the earliest botanical gardens: The one in Padua, for instance, kept its exotic plantings in their appropriate compass direction. Circular in design, it placed flowers from the south in the south, eastern trees in the east, and so forth. Here the physical world was quite literally re-created.

*Fig. 31   This astonishing example of seventeenth-century Florentine* pietra
dura *(a mosaic of "hard stone") shows one of the Cabinets of Curiosities so
popular at the time. Among the displays are pictures, stones, medals, plants,
and intricately carved ivories—what today might be called collectibles.*

The experts whose investigations made such collections
possible, the antiquarians, came to be regarded as the most
learned scholars of their time. It is no coincidence that the first
half of the seventeenth century, when the mania for the Cabinet of Curiosities reached its height, reports of wonders from
distant lands, studies of coins and inscriptions, and the mining
of texts attracted the finest minds. Those who became adepts of
universal knowledge were highly regarded, though many of the
most renowned, such as the learned Provençal gentleman

Fig. 32   Hans Hoff-
mann's 1589 painting of a
reindeer head with mon-
strous horns was done in
Prague for Emperor Rudolf
II, the greatest collector of
curiosities of the age.

Nicolas de Peiresc, are known today only to a few specialists.
Peiresc conducted a gigantic correspondence that embraced
the elite of Europe's letters and arts, and he addressed just
about every issue deemed to be important in the world of ideas
in his day. When Louis XIII needed expert advice on arcane
historical issues, it was to Peiresc that he turned.

Because Peiresc never published a word, his name does not
loom as large as those of his many friends and admirers, such
as Hugo Grotius, William Camden, or his biographer Pierre
Gassendi. But for them he was a point of reference, and in
many respects the central intellectual figure of the age. What set
him apart was not only his indefatigable erudition and his quest
for every possible kind of knowledge but also his devotion to
the exchange of information and his determination to ground

all values in the wisdom of the past. His learning was intended to be openly available for the betterment of mankind, and his irenicism and his commitment to Stoicism were seen as promoting a new kind of moral uprightness.

Here was one way of reestablishing order in a Europe torn apart by doubt and self-laceration. If all information and all material substance could be comprehended, maybe one could rise above the quarrels and the dislocations. Might one be able to overwhelm the unease with a supreme effort of total understanding and control, which could bring all creation and all history within one's grasp?

The same impulse was at work in the creation of a remarkable new art form in these very years: opera. Here was another means of expressing the ambition to achieve universality. For opera promised some of the same rewards as the *omnium gatherum*. It brought together every known means of creativity—poetry, music, dance, painting, sculpture, and architecture—in a gigantic, united effort to subdue the senses. No form of expression remained unused in the attempt to sweep audiences into enthusiastic assent. Moreover, the great city where opera first flourished, Venice, also devised the special structure that best captured its qualities: the high hall, ringed with tiers of boxes, that became the opera house. The inspiration for the subject matter was, as usual, antiquity: Composers sought to recapture the presentations in song and dance that were believed to have been integral to Greek drama (figs. 33 and 34). And the subjects that were treated by the form's most brilliant pioneer, Monteverdi—Orpheus, Ulysses, Nero—were taken from the ancient world. Opera was the final flourish of the Renaissance, a last resort to the inspiration of antiquity in order to address the concerns of a particular time. As it fashioned an

*Figs. 33 and 34 (facing page)    Built in the Venetian city of Vicenza by Andrea Palladio in 1584, the Teatro Olimpico is the only surviving theater from the Renaissance. None of the opera houses that were soon to be built has survived, but one can see in this contemporary auditorium that Palladio's design is almost an object lesson in the influence of antiquity: The amphitheatre follows Greek and Roman models, as do the columns and statuary at the back; and the permanent stage set is a marvel of trompe l'oeil perspective using buildings in the classical style.*

all-encompassing vision of the world, it constructed order where there was none.

❦

As the sense of crisis mounted in the sixteenth century, it was echoed by the prevailing style in painting and sculpture, Mannerism. During the fifteenth century, artists who followed Petrarch's lead in imitating antiquity had mastered perspective and

the depiction of the natural world. By the early 1500s they had achieved a calm assurance, and were able to convey the serenity that we associate, above all, with that exemplar of the High Renaissance, Raphael. But after Raphael died in 1520, things began to change. Unsettling distortions appeared, with a new focus on agonized figures and swirling, unstable compositions. The new style that took hold, Mannerism, reflected uncannily the troubling uncertainties of these post-1520 years. The Michelangelo slaves struggling to free themselves from their marble bonds; the Parmigianino figures given inexplicable gestures and odd postures; the disturbing subjects of Titian's late masterpieces; the baffling compositions and elongated figures of El Greco: All seemed symptomatic of a world in which doubts were growing and answers remained elusive (figs. 35 and 36).

*Fig. 35  The story of Marsyas, the musician who challenged Apollo and was flayed as punishment, inspired the aged Titian in the 1570s to create this haunting scene, rendered even more gruesome by the dog lapping Marsyas' blood. The contrast with the sunny atmosphere of his early work, some seventy years before, could hardly be stronger.*

But just as the antiquarians and the opera composers sought to subjugate uncertainty with comprehensive displays of knowledge and creativity, so too did Baroque artists, from the 1590s onward, shift gears and try to overwhelm their

*Fig. 36 El Greco's* Resurrec-
tion, *painted circa 1605–1610,
is an example not only of deep
piety but also of the distortions,
the artificial poses, and the unsettling compositions that were
characteristic of mannerism.*

viewers with power and emotion. They were still inspired by
the ancient world, but they now left behind the hesitations
and bewilderments of the Mannerists and instead exuded
self-confidence and grandeur. Their forte was the depiction
of moments of high drama. Enormous canvases, spectacular

buildings, brilliant colors, and powerful figures swept all who beheld them into a state of awe and acquiescence. This was the style, above all, of absolutist princes and the patrons of the Counter-Reformation Church, who relished the Baroque's assertiveness and its ability to dazzle and inspire.

One has but to stand in St. Peter's Square, surrounded by Bernini's massive colonnade, to see how effective such propaganda could be (fig. 23). The stunning portraits of the rulers of the time, whether by van Dyck or by Velázquez, were no less overwhelming. And the huge canvases by Rubens, glorifying Habsburgs, Stuarts, and Bourbons alike (figs. 42 and 43), not to mention his stirring religious scenes, merely confirm how all-pervasive were the aspirations of his time. It was a determined campaign to conquer the questions, the uncertainties, that bedeviled Europe during the first half of the seventeenth century.

❧

But the attempt was to fail. Ever since the crucial decades surrounding 1500, the problems of political and other kinds of change had gradually intensified and no means of restoring stability and certainty had appeared. Europeans would have to move on, to new assumptions and expectations. When that at last began to happen, they found themselves at the dawn of the last days of the Renaissance.

*Chapter Five*

# THE LAST DAYS OF
# THE RENAISSANCE

S ome seventy years ago, Paul Hazard published the book
that, more than any other, has defined the way we think
about the process that brought the culture of the Renaissance to
an end: *La Crise de la conscience européenne*. Focusing on the last
decades of the seventeenth century and the early years of the
eighteenth, Hazard argued that, around 1700, a new level of
skepticism, a new willingness to move beyond the authority of
the past, and a new commitment to the power of systematic and
reasoned thought created a culture of innovation and challenge
markedly different from that of the previous age. Although the
people and ideas he focused on have attracted a great deal of attention in the interim, the basic story he told has not been superseded. It now seems possible to expand on his insights, and
to make more comprehensive the claim that the second half of
the seventeenth century marked the end of an era.

In the previous pages we have given attention to various aspects of the history of the period from the mid-fourteenth to the mid-seventeenth centuries. We have outlined the coherences that bound the era together, and we have followed the tensions that gradually, starting around 1500, brought Europeans by the 1640s to a realization that traditional norms and structures were under attack: that the order and cultural unity they had taken for granted might not hold. Assumptions and practices that had been in place for centuries now dissolved in an age of unrelenting crisis. This was a period, extending for some two decades starting in the 1640s, of intense conflict. Central to the disorder of the time were political and social upheavals that ranged from revolution in England to civil wars in Spain, France, eastern Europe, and Italy, coups d'etat in the Netherlands and Sweden, and uprisings in cities as disparate as Barcelona, Bordeaux, Naples, Amsterdam, and Königsberg. Only the exhaustion as the Thirty Years' War came to an end saved central Europe from similar confrontations between rulers and subjects, though the violence and suffering of the previous decades had given the inhabitants of those areas more than a taste of the struggles that swept through Europe in the 1640s and 1650s.

It is clear that, from the 1660s onward, as Europeans began to resolve the issues that had led to the crisis, fundamental shifts of structure and outlook gradually emerged: A new set of unities, a new era, began to crystallize. In politics, in society, in economic affairs, and in the culture at large, different relationships were forming. The landmarks of the previous centuries no longer pointed the way; a new age was taking shape. Since the time of Hazard, these decades have been much investigated. The British historian G. N. Clark used the metaphor of the watershed to describe the years around 1650; and a series of contributors to the journal *Past & Present* explored at great length the elements of what they called the "crisis" of the mid-century. Even if one does not try to touch on every aspect of the transformation that these studies have uncovered, one can see how the verities of Renaissance culture gave way to a new order.

⤳

The arena of fiercest upheaval was politics, where the long-festering conflict between regional autonomy and centralizing governments finally erupted into violence in the 1640s. Ever since the fall of the Roman Empire, localities and their dominant lords had been the prime units of political authority and organization. For Renaissance Europe, even as bureaucracy and military capacity shifted the balance of power toward kings and princes, it had remained axiomatic that a city or a province handled its own affairs. By the mid-seventeenth century, however, that equilibrium had been irreparably undermined.

What linked just about all the battles of the 1640s and 1650s, not to mention the sieges princes had to conduct against their own cities—most notably Barcelona and Bordeaux, Amsterdam and Königsberg—was a determination to assert uniform control over territories that had long relished their independence. Powerful resistance to that effort prompted the political crisis of these decades. The significance of the outcome of that crisis, which became clear by the last decades of the seventeenth century, was that it did indeed bring the struggles to an end. Though grudging, there was a general acceptance throughout Europe that a new order had been put into place. It took many different forms, but everywhere certain elements could be seen that set this "modern" structure apart from Renaissance regimes.

The overarching framework, unprecedented in its scope, was the series of international agreements hammered out in Westphalia in the 1640s. Not since the end of Roman hegemony around the year 400 had there been a set of agreed principles that determined the relations among rulers throughout Europe. From Moscow to Madrid, the Westphalia treaties were greeted as the bedrock of a new stability, and that is what they proved to be. As late as the negotiations for the Versailles treaties of 1815 and 1918, the boundary-drawing and dispute-settling that preoccupied these congresses harked back, in essence, to 1648. And the basic procedures of diplomacy, developed during the Renaissance, now became the standardized means of international communication. The years of discussion it took to produce the Westphalia treaties, the comprehensiveness of the topics they covered, and the breadth of participation they embraced combined to create a system of precedents and procedures that had not existed before, and was to remain in effect throughout the age that followed. Symptomatic of the shift that had taken place was *On the Manner of Negotiating with Princes* by Louis de Callières, a work that was able to sum up the new situation in 1716.

Nobody claimed that warfare would cease just because a new diplomatic structure had been created. But it is noticeable that, as the interests of states rather than religious passions became the occasions for war, the brutality that had been evident in the Thirty Years' War became less marked. As regimes began to realize how important for their own ends it was to preserve civilian economies and not let marauding soldiers loose, troops

*Fig. 37    The regularization of military life as armies became ever larger made common sights of the military academy, the parade ground, and soldiers drilling, as we see in this French engraving of the eighteenth century.*

came under tighter discipline. As part of the effort to restrain the excesses of armed conflict, massive building programs, notably in France, made it possible to house armies in barracks rather than billeting them on the population; at the same time, the development of reliable supplies of food and clothing cut down on looting. Finally, by founding military academies, states could regulate their soldiers' behavior directly, establishing rules for warfare and ensuring that drill and training became the norm for recruits (fig. 37).

It was also significant that, for more than a century, warfare was to be provoked by territorial aggrandizement or economic ambition, purely political objectives. Not until the first stirrings of national feeling in the age of the French Revolution did the ferocity characteristic of the religious wars return to the European scene. Moreover, this basic shift in the attitude toward armed conflict was foretold (as we will see in the next chapter) in the work of some of society's most perceptive and prescient figures, its artists. Their ability to advance an antiwar message, after millennia of admiration for the warrior, was an unmistakable sign of a fundamental reorientation in European culture.

Indicative of the new international and military system was the growing interest in such geopolitical notions as the balance of power. Rulers with common enemies had joined forces before, but now they cooperated to form alliances with pan-European goals. The first to feel the effects of this larger perspective was Louis XIV, whose aggressions were met by the formation of an alliance that, unlike previous such assemblages, was essentially defensive. The Holy League of the early sixteenth century, for example, had come together for aggressive purposes: to drive the Ottoman Turks from the Mediterranean. By contrast, the League of Augsburg in the 1680s sought primarily to hold back an expanding France. Louis observed the new niceties by assembling elaborate legal opinions in support of his claims to territory, but his neighbors took a more comprehensive view of Europe's frontiers: To preserve a balance and an order that they believed he was seeking to overturn, they fought him to a standstill. The resulting "system of alliances" held sway in Europe until World War I, surviving such "shocks" as the so-called diplomatic revolution of 1740—when individual shifts led to a wholesale rearrangement of continent-wide alliances—and the later assaults on accepted conventions associated with Napoleon and the independence movements of the nineteenth century.

Within polities the new stability was also apparent. For all the differences among individual states, the essential components did not vary. The centuries-old tension between local autonomies and centralizing forces had reached definitive resolution with the triumph of the center. What this required was the final subjugation of the three major rivals who, since the early Middle Ages, had been the chief alternative sources of authority against whom kings and princes had had to struggle: the aristocracy, the cities, and the Church.

The process of state-building had been largely directed at all three. But it was not until the last third or so of the seventeenth century that governments could feel secure in their triumph. The most remarkable of the alliances that now crystallized was the deepening partnership between the nobility and the center. We saw in Chapter 3 that the "domestication" of the aristocracy began in the Renaissance, largely in response to specific consequences of gunpowder warfare: first, the destruction of the capacity for resistance of the lord's usual last line of defense, his castle; and second, the removal (by long-distance killing) of the traditional justification for noble status, namely, courage in armed combat. The result was a transformation in the self-image of the gentleman: He now set himself apart from his inferiors not just through his valor but also by his courtly skills, his refinement, and his education. Not that he valued his ability to lead any the less; he now displayed that quality by his ability to rule as a great landowner rather than a knight. The final stage of "domestication" came when he realized that he could shine most brightly in this regard by exercising his authority *through* central government rather than against it. Maintaining the centuries-old struggle against the prince was futile. If one couldn't fight him, one joined him.

The results were everywhere to be seen. As central governments established their control throughout their realms, the crucial administrators they relied on were those great men who were accustomed to command and now had the education and administrative skills to take on this vital role. The extreme example was on display in Vienna, where the Habsburg emperor, Leopold I, appointed as ministers or generals a succession of aristocrats who were not even native to his lands: Ottavio Piccolomini, Charles of Lorraine, Eugène of Savoy. But the basic relationship was apparent in all of Europe's capital cities.

Sharp distinctions used to be drawn between the absolutist and the "constitutionalist" regimes that emerged in the late seventeenth century. The former, revolving around a potent ruler, answerable to no one but God, rode roughshod over the rights of the subject; the latter, dependent on consent and cooperation, paid heed to the needs of its citizens. But the distinction no longer holds much force. Differences certainly remained: Whereas in France and Spain it was the rights of a community or region that were still defended, in England it was the rights of the individual. But the alliance between central governments and provincial elites was at the heart of all the new bureaucratic regimes.

Whether it was the gentry in England or the nobles of robe or sword in France, the point was the same. There was far more to be gained through government service than by hanging on to local rights. It has been shown in recent years how vital to the "absolutist" system in France was the cooperation of local nobles, who had found that they protected their privileges and incomes more effectively by serving the monarchy than by opposing it. The classic instance was the Prince of Condé, a grandee with royal blood, who earlier in life had been forced into exile because of rebellion against the crown, but who ended his days rowing ladies on the lake at Versailles.

The pattern was repeated in England. The great confrontation between Parliament and monarch in the 1640s and 1650s might have ended in victory for the former, but the march of centralization hardly missed a step. On the surface, Parliament in England certainly seemed supreme, as impervious to outside influence as the absolutist monarchy in France. For both, however, the first impression disguised the reality that the true ruler of the land was an alliance between elite and monarchy. The English gentry might have been able to use their control of Parliament to override royal will, but the need did not arise. Indeed, when James II tried to flout the wishes of his subjects in the late 1680s, they expelled him in a bloodless "Glorious" Revolution, thus demonstrating that subject and king had no choice but to work together.

By and large, the average landowner was content to allow those who ran the country from London to get on with it, knowing that his interests would be represented. During the next century, England's bureaucracy grew enormously; political parties took shape; elections were disputed by the few who could vote; and new structures of government arose, including the development of the office of prime minister, responsible to Parliament, and the emergence of the notion of cabinet responsibility. All this change, though, took place in the context of a close working relationship between monarchs and gentry. That in the long run this proved to be a more stable system, especially when supported by the more even-handed legal procedures of the common law and by the most successful economy in Europe, was confirmed when England avoided the revolutions that ravaged the Continent at the end of the eighteenth century. The fundamental cooperation between provincial elite and national capital, however, was much the same; it was the major reason that the centralization achieved in the seventeenth century was not only universal but also essentially unchallenged until the separatist movements of the twentieth century.

When one describes this political structure as the *ancien regime*, that is precisely what it remained, throughout Europe, for the next 250 years. An inherited aristocracy, after centuries of struggle, was in control of government and society, disturbed only by occasional incursions from below. The growing importance of economic affairs meant merely that commercial success offered entry into that aristocracy. The alliance between business and politics was closest and most productive in England and the Netherlands, the two countries that recovered most quickly from the dislocations of the seventeenth century, but eventually it was generally recognized that the cozy relationship was essential if a regime was to be fully effective. The founding of the Bank of Amsterdam in 1609 and, even more notably, the Bank of England in 1694 made it clear that the success of a government was intimately linked to a country's economy and thus to its financial leadership. It came to be assumed that the state would support the interests of its commercial class, and the latter responded in kind. The rather different situation in the Ottoman Empire, where the political elite in Constantinople had little interaction with the business elite in Smyrna, proved to be a blueprint for stagnation.

In the West, by contrast, cities had ceased to struggle for their autonomy after the mid-seventeenth-century crisis, and their integration into centralized government (like that of the aristocracy) proved beneficial on every side. Merchants could shape policy to suit their interests, and regimes gained taxes and support from a vital sector of society. That all churches had by now become subservient to nonreligious interests merely confirmed that a new structure was in place, one that surely would have amazed and delighted many a Renaissance prince.

⤳

There was only one significant exception to this pattern, but it helps make the point. What set the late seventeenth century apart in intellectual life was the definitive assertion by writers and philosophers, for the first time since the Renaissance began, that the moderns might know more or be better than the ancients. This rejection of the very essence of the culture of the age had its political counterpart in the actions of a monarch of terrifying and ruthless energy, Peter the Great of Russia, who sought to impose that very view on the government, economic behavior, and society of his realm. Unlike his fellow rulers, he disdained the need for cooperation with his elites, but his indifference—though unique at the time—confirmed how complete was the break with a past of struggle between center and province.

Peter the Great was in a league of his own amongst the centralizing rulers of his age. Although his contemporaries in France, Austria, Prussia, and Sweden were often breaking new ground in their quest for centralized powers—raising taxes, expanding bureaucracies, imposing tighter controls over their subjects' lives, and pursuing aggressive foreign policies—none had his fierce determination to break with the past. Indeed, the image cultivated by every one of the innovative political leaders of the period we have covered was that they were doing nothing new. When the Huguenots were tearing France apart in the 1560s and 1570s, their theorist François Hotman argued that they were merely restoring the consultative rule that had first been devised by the ancient Gauls. Their contemporaries, the Dutch who were rebelling against Philip II of Spain, claimed that the king had trampled on ancient rights. Similarly, the English revolutionaries of the mid-seventeenth century asserted that they were merely seeking to remove the yoke cast upon England by the Normans. Oliver Cromwell repeatedly insisted (and we have no reason to doubt him) that he sought no more than a restoration of the values of his fellow country gentlemen in the face of tyranny:

> As far as I can, I am ready to serve that cause not as a King, but as a Constable. I have thought often that I could not tell what my business was save comparing myself to a good Constable, keeping the peace of the parish. Truly, this has been my satisfaction in the troubles I have undergone. God has so dealt with Kings that he blasted the title. I will not build Jericho again.

Cromwell's very title, Protector, proclaimed his wish to conserve rather than eradicate. And each time Louis XIV, for all of his aggressions, set his eyes on a new slice of territory, he solicited from his legal experts the documentation to justify his annexation as mere recovery for France of a long-denied possession.

Peter made no such excuses. On the contrary. To him, the past was anathema. Every reform he instituted was an attempt to erase the traditions that, in his view, were holding Russia back and preventing her from achieving the power and status she deserved. Louis XIV built himself a magnificent new palace at Versailles as a setting for his government, but Peter

*Fig. 38 It is ironic that, when Catherine the Great commissioned Étienne-Maurice Falconnet in the 1760s to create Peter the Great's chief monument in St. Petersburg, it portrayed the czar, who had so determinedly turned his back on the past, as a Roman hero.*

(fig. 38) built himself an entire city, and he called it after his own name saint, St. Petersburg—a gesture that evoked the one precedent for such self-glorification in western history, Alexander the Great and Alexandria.

The czar did not enjoy the same military genius as Alexander, but he was no less contemptuous of convention, no less prepared to destroy tradition, and no less determined to bulldoze his way to a new world. From the forced shaving of beards to the founding of an Academy of Sciences, Peter wanted nothing so much as a radical reordering of Russian society and culture. There has perhaps been no king in history who so relentlessly—and brutally, if necessary—insisted that as many traces of the past as possible be wiped out. It was with little concern for the distress he might cause (an indifference that sometimes, as in the murder of his own son, echoed the callousness of Ivan the Terrible) that he put his decisions into effect. He moved the capital from Moscow to St. Petersburg, in the process causing the deaths of thousands as workers raced to complete the new city in the marshes at the mouth of the Neva River; he created a navy where none had been before; he made government office, not family inheritance, the mark of nobility; he brought the church under royal control; he opened xenophobic Russia to a flood of western engineers, architects, soldiers, and artists; he imposed central power through a bureaucracy of such unprecedented complexity that it saturated the country from then onward; and he initiated fundamental reforms in just about every institution he could lay his hands on. For all the benefits they brought, his policies created tensions in Russian society that have persisted ever since: Was the West to be welcomed or rejected; might change improve the lot of the ordinary person, or were hopes always to be dashed (an attitude summed up by those who, in the depths of a St. Petersburg winter, describe the climate as nine months of expectation followed by three months of disappointment)? But that Peter brought about a decisive break with the past was undeniable.

Other monarchs may have attempted some part of his wholesale overhaul. Philip II of Spain, for instance, had created a new capital in Madrid in the late sixteenth century. Kings during the Reformation had won control of their churches.

And Louis XIV in France and Charles II in England gave to scientific societies a stamp of royal approval that was essential not only to the new prestige of the scientist but also to the cultural transformation that science brought about. But no king had ever launched a set of reforms that even approached in range and depth what Peter now set in motion. One cannot imagine another court in Europe, of this period or any other, accepting, advancing, and showering honors on a black African, Abram Petrovich Ganibal, the great-grandfather of Alexander Pushkin. Peter's break with the past was of titanic proportions, and although much of his effort was in emulation of western models, the very thoroughness of the czar's eradication of the old makes him the equivalent in politics of Isaac Newton in science.

∞

If the second half of the seventeenth century witnessed the last days of Renaissance politics, both international and domestic, and also the final settlement of social and economic relations into new patterns, so too did it mark a fundamental shift in the view of the supernatural. Nothing was more basic to the outlook of an individual in medieval and Renaissance Europe than the sense of a spiritual realm that lay beyond rational comprehension. How else could one explain day-to-day events? The works of Hieronymus Bosch (fig. 39) sought to visualize the devils and demons who hover over humanity at all times and tempt us and punish us throughout our lives. And in a multitude of artistic works one could see the angels who represented the more positive aspirations of mankind. From the few who, it was believed, could look into this hidden realm—mystics, prophets, witches, astrologers—much was expected. They

*Fig. 39   The demons flying through the sky of Bosch's* Temptation of St. An-
thony *(1500), carrying off damned souls, make visible the evil spirits and devils who were assumed to be present everywhere, constantly assaulting mankind.*

could foretell the future; they could explain why a child fell ill;
they could give the lesser mortals around them a path into the
hidden world that controlled human destiny.

Such beliefs—recently labeled "superstition"—persist today, but there is a major difference. Individuals and groups
may accept them, but they do not have the official standing
they were granted in medieval and Renaissance times. And that
crucial loss of standing happened in exactly this period. The
shift took place even though signs, portents, and the mystical
numerical significance of the year 1666—derived from apocalyptic passages in the Bible that implied that the number 666

heralded the end of the world—seemed for a while only to intensify the interest in the supernatural. The next chapter will deal further with this fundamental reorientation of outlook, but it deserves emphasis here as an indicator of the sea-change through which European culture passed in the middle decades of the seventeenth century. Indeed, one could argue that the turning away from the all-pervasive power of the supernatural that happened at this time ensured that the new era that was coming into being was unlike any that had ever come before.

⤚

The next elements in our story come from the more systematic and rational arenas of the world of ideas, and their reflection in the arts. It could be argued that here was the source of all the other changes that overtook Europe during the second half of the seventeenth century. Those who regard the steady advance of rationalism as the underlying theme of western history, or who assume that the Scientific Revolution triumphed because the new picture of nature that it offered was more "correct" than the old one, would suggest that the decisive breakthroughs of the period were in these areas, and the rest followed. That one can recognize the shifts in scholarship, in philosophy, in theology, and in the study of nature as being autonomous, explicable within the confines of each of these fields, is not, however, to give any of them a uniquely causative importance. The enthusiasm for the new science certainly had broad effects. But one has to see that victory as itself a product of the times, a response to the yearning for assurance and stability after more than a century of uncertainty and doubt. The rise of science was not self-evident; it was just one symptom of the fundamental re-thinkings of the age. Like the transformations of political and social relations, of the attitude toward the supernatural, and of ideas and arts, it was part of the profound change in outlook that took Europe out of the Renaissance.

One of the earliest casualties was antiquarianism. A recent study of the most famous of the antiquarians of the early seventeenth century, the Frenchman Nicolas Peiresc, whose massive correspondence with colleagues throughout Europe provided the armature underlying the entire enterprise, raised the question of why a form of inquiry that was so highly valued in Peiresc's lifetime should so soon have become disregarded after his death in 1637. Why did the impulse that had driven these learned men, had permeated their scholarship, and had made them famous begin to take on the marginal and slightly comical image it has retained to this day? There were hints of what was to come even in Peiresc's lifetime, notably in John Donne's epigram:

> *If in his study he hath so much care*
> *To hang all old strange things,*
> *Let his wife beware.*

But Peiresc would have been shocked to see the writings of John Aubrey, a younger contemporary who shared many of his interests, performed as a comic turn on the London stage, as they were a few years ago. Unshakeable seriousness, and a conviction that the recovery of all knowledge was essential to the political, religious, and intellectual health of society, was central to his life's work. As he put it, "I find everywhere some little thing from which I can glean and profit."

The trouble was that, as an aura of self-assurance returned to European culture, so too did an unease with what seemed excessive seriousness; it was symptomatic that the reaction against religious extremes was a denunciation of enthusiasm. Yet that was exactly the quality that the antiquarians had prized. No sharper contrast to their emphasis on substance could be imagined than the superficial salon culture that took hold of Paris in the 1630s and began to shape intellectual life. The salons, dedicated to displays of elegance, wit, and light conversation (the third-rate poet Voiture, for instance, was considered more of a star guest than the great playwright Corneille) had no place for the earnestness, hard work, and dedication of the antiquary. Run by aristocrats—often the "learned ladies" whom Molière was to satirize in *Les Femmes Savantes*—the salons, increasingly the arbiters of cultural fashion, emphasized grace and repartee, and had little time for the dour figure of the antiquary.

This was the main casualty of the burst of frivolity that arose as the crisis of mid-century died away. The new lightness in the culture—spawned, no doubt, by relief that the tensions of the preceding decades had subsided—was apparent not merely at the French salons. It was noticeable, too, in the change of mood between the gravity of John Milton's stately poetry, which sought the epic qualities of antiquity, and John Dryden's clever, acerbic verse, which poked fun at the poet's contemporaries; and between the towering ambitions of Baroque masters such as Rubens and Velázquez, still struggling with religious and mythological scenes, and the gentler purposes of Rococo artists such as Watteau (see plate 8); and even in the progression from the harsh pessimism of Thomas Hobbes to the reassuring optimism of John Locke. One can see the future coming in the quieter canvases of Dutch masters, notably Vermeer, and in the growing attention by painters to landscape, still life, and similar less fraught subjects, but the subsidence of the heroic and the intensely devout in art was far from complete at mid-century. Moreover, it is hard to claim that the Renaissance was over as long as Milton, the last great figure in the Homeric tradition, remained at work, and indeed his death in 1674 can be seen as a marker in the change of eras. The contrast between the classically inclined, ever-struggling, and highly serious ambitions embodied in Milton, and the lowered sights, fondness for glitter, and gentler atmosphere and purpose that animated the writers of the next generation was unmistakable.

A symptom of the transition was the widespread decline in the seriousness of university education. It is interesting that this should have happened at the very time when attitudes toward the instruction of the young were entering a new era. John Locke's *Some Thoughts Concerning Education,* published in 1693, was the first major call for an end to the traditional reliance on harshness when dealing with children. Encouragement, he argued, was far more effective than punishment, and the future indeed lay with nurture rather than the repressive regime that had long ruled classroom and home. At universities, however, after the great surge of enrollments during the Renaissance, attendance leveled off, stagnation descended, and there was a noticeable drop-off in scholarly attainments and intellectual standards. This is not to suggest that we are coming from unmitigated dourness into pure frivolity. Deftness and wit were plentiful during the Renaissance, but the conspicuous turn to these values in the late seventeenth century can be regarded as a sign that the transition from the anxieties of the previous decades was complete.

A good part of the reason for the widespread feeling that long-standing quarrels had died away was the decline in confessional disputes. Through the early days of the Thirty Years' War, foreign policies had often been driven by religious animosities (notably in the era when Philip II's Spain had seen as its mission the advance of Christianity, and in particular the fortunes of the Roman Church). But the unprecedented alliance between Catholic France and Protestant Sweden in the early 1630s, at the height of the Thirty Years' War, made it clear that confessional aims no longer held the influence over foreign policies that they had enjoyed since the Reformation. By the 1650s, the devout Puritan Oliver Cromwell was debating whether he should ally himself with Catholic Spain or Catholic France, and he was fighting a war against his fellow Protestants, the Dutch. Henceforth, political and economic considerations dominated international affairs.

The subsidence of these passions was to a large extent the result of a growing realization that the lines dividing Protestant from Catholic areas in Europe had become relatively stable. The various churches had consolidated their hold over the territories they dominated, and although acts of intolerance were still to come—notably the expulsion from France of its Protestant minority in 1685—by and large Europeans had come to accept the geographic distribution of the faiths. The churches had, in turn, defined creeds, established lines of authority, and in general established order within their ranks. A new and more stable structure for religious practice had been put in place, and it was signaled by a major shift in the image of the Jesuits. Once thought of as the Church's shock troops, dedicated to the eradication of heresy, they now conducted their missionary work mainly overseas. Within Europe itself, their reputation was increasingly based on the excellence of the educational institutions they had founded.

What this development made possible was an unprecedented (though grudging) acceptance of the principle of religious toleration. The cause had had its advocates in the sixteenth century: Erasmus; Sebastian Castellio; a pragmatic group concerned about disorder, the *politiques,* in France; Michel de Montaigne and Jean Bodin; and an English advocate of coexistence, Edwin Sandys. But these had been voices in the wilderness. In the late seventeenth century, such sentiments entered the mainstream. Beyond the powerful advocates—John Milton, Pierre Bayle, John Locke—there were formal policies that overturned past attitudes. In Rhode Island, an entire society embraced the principle; and in Europe, the implicit acceptance of religious minorities became the norm. Each country still had its official religion, which bestowed privileges of public office and higher education on its adherents, but England's Act of Toleration, passed by Parliament in 1689, was the wave of the future. This change would probably have been as startling as any in the post-1660 world to the people of Renaissance Europe.

Two other aspects of religious life deserve mention. First was the decline in accusations of witchcraft. By the late seventeenth century, the process that has been called the "disenchantment of the world" was well under way. The notion that there was a hidden purpose to everything that happened, that the world was "enchanted," and that witches and others knew how to manipulate it, was eroding as rapidly as the more general supernatural beliefs discussed above. Various explanations for the change have been offered: the rise of science, the increased use of practical measures to defend against disaster (such as firefighting services and insurance), and the tightening professional standards (and skepticism) applied by lawyers, clergymen, and doctors to claims of magical behavior. One remarkable consequence of the new, practically-minded approach to natural disasters was the elimination, after some 350 years, of the worst ravages of the scourge that had shadowed the Renaissance, plague. Thanks to aggressive government enforcements of quarantine—a notable instance took place in Marseilles in 1720—the spread of the disease was limited, and local outbreaks did not become Europe-wide epidemics.

A lessening of fear helped mitigate witchcraft hysteria, and in this regard the most decisive influence may have been the calming down after the crisis of mid-century: With anxiety levels lower, there was less reason to seek scapegoats for ill fortune. In addition, the uneasiness about excessive passion of a war-weary Europe undoubtedly fueled the reaction against the disruptions of witchcraft accusations. Whatever the reason, the pattern was clear, and paralleled again the shift in cultural norms that marked the last days of the Renaissance.

In one other respect the scenery was becoming unfamiliar. It was in these years that the first hints began to emerge of a seismic shift in the belief system that had seemed beyond question ever since Christianity had conquered Europe. For the first time, religious faith itself came under fire. This startling leap into a possibly godless world did not happen overnight. The word "atheist" remained a term of abuse for many decades to come (it was a favorite slander used by critics of Hobbes). But by the second half of the seventeenth century, various indications appeared of what was to come. In his writings in the 1650s, for instance, the Dutch philosopher Baruch Spinoza was openly scathing about divine influence in earthly matters. Though he certainly believed in the existence of God, his conception of the deity has been summed up as "a God who is not separate from his creation, who has no anthropomorphic properties, who is not concerned with the fate of humanity, who is not a lawgiver or judge, and whose power is manifested in a deterministic universe." No Christian (or Jewish) believer could have regarded those views as anything but a travesty of religion, and Spinoza was fortunate to have been merely cursed and excommunicated by the Jewish community of Amsterdam: If he had been a nominal Christian in some areas of Europe, he would have suffered a far more unpleasant fate. In one recent account, his sweeping reassessment of the human lot has been described as the root of the egalitarian and secularist views promoted by the radical thinkers of the Enlightenment in the next century.

More generally, the reaction against "enthusiasm" and passion in the wake of the Thirty Years' War took some of the earlier concerns of skepticism and Stoicism in new directions. Even the Jesuit-trained Descartes had begun his investigation of knowledge with the mind rather than with God, and it soon became acceptable to emphasize reason rather than faith as a guide to perception and thought. But there were also some specific nudges in this direction.

One arose as a result of the continuing quarrels between the religious faiths, which, though now conducted mainly through publications, not warfare, had a notable unintended consequence. For among the tactics of the theologians who took up these polemics in the mid- and late-seventeenth century was the habit of taking their opponents' positions to a logical extreme and then suggesting that such views led implicitly to atheism. Once the possibility arose that a particular view might indeed lead to atheism, the notion attracted attention and further study. The result was that, eventually, a mere polemical device began to lay the groundwork for the acceptance of deism, and even atheism, in the eighteenth century.

The same effect was to follow from the new understanding of the nature of the Bible that scholars started to develop at this very time, in the mid-seventeenth century. Both Thomas Hobbes in England and Baruch Spinoza in the Netherlands questioned the Mosaic authorship of the Hebrew Bible, and their questions were vastly amplified, in 1678, by the publication of the first systematic examination of the Bible as a historical text, the work of the Frenchman Richard Simon. The interpretations put forward by Simon, the founder of a branch of scholarship now known as the Higher Criticism, were based on an analysis of the parallel narratives and repetitions in the Hebrew Bible. Although his conclusions were to be superseded, his basic method remained a powerful influence on discussions of the Bible. What made it sensational was its suggestion that the holy text was not simply a record of divine inspiration but rather a man-made document. Thus was removed yet another foundation of traditional religious belief.

Not long thereafter, an even more radical and notorious assault was launched on the long-held and comfortable assumptions of the age. An anonymous tract known as "The Three Impostors" claimed that Moses, Christ, and Mohammed had all been false prophets. A false Messiah, in the shape of the Jewish visionary Shabtai Zvi, had recently been exposed as a sham, and now the doubts were extended to the very foundations of religion. These were still fringe ideas, and were long to remain so; but their emergence at this time was a telling indication that the Renaissance, and much of what it had stood for, had come to an end.

❧

The final piece in the creation of the new age was the change in the ways of examining and understanding nature that is known as the Scientific Revolution. For many students of the period this has seemed to be the decisive blow that demolished the central Renaissance belief in the superiority of antiquity. It certainly was crucial to that fundamental shift: It was the clearest proof that the moderns had outdone the ancients. The very acceptance of the new science, however, reflected a larger quest for assurance and order—a context in which even this major step becomes one among many marks of the passing of Renaissance culture.

Still, the importance of the triumph of Newtonianism, and all it stood for, is hard to overstate. Even as the explorers of nature had laid the groundwork, during the Renaissance, for the dramatically changed methods and ideas that emerged in the seventeenth century, they had insisted on their reverence for the masters of antiquity. Thus, although his arguments were to leave the principles of Aristotelian physics in ruins, Galileo regularly paid his respects to Aristotle himself. Soon after Galileo's death in 1642, however, it became clear that, in astronomy and anatomy no less than in physics, a picture of the world was being formed that was incompatible with the image that had held sway in classrooms and writings for nearly two thousand years.

For us, the achievements of the scientists of the sixteenth and seventeenth centuries have about them an air of inevitability. But the condemnation of Galileo by the Inquisition in 1633 is an indication of the uncertainties the pioneers faced as they sought to transform long-held assumptions about the natural world. Nicolaus Copernicus never sought to publish his findings; they appeared in print, thanks to a friend's efforts, when he was on his deathbed, and they immediately provoked derision from those who saw them as contradicting the Bible. Johannes Kepler was repeatedly in trouble with the authorities, mainly for religious reasons, and it is worth recalling that a lost copy of a manuscript draft of his *Somnium*—a speculation about the nature of a voyage to the moon that begins with the traveler's mother conjuring up a "daemon"—might have encouraged the trial of his real mother as a witch. William Harvey's discovery of the circulatory system had little immediate effect on investigations of the human body. And René Descartes hesitated before publishing one of his works, fearful of condemnation in the wake of Galileo's trial.

The acceptance of the new ideas in the second half of the seventeenth century was the result not of intellectual debate but of a shift in mood. A culture seeking an end to the atmosphere of doubt and uncertainty that had prevailed for decades turned to these confident investigators, who were making such decisive claims to truth, and adopted them wholeheartedly. Science became fashionable, the entertainment of choice at country house parties, and for intellectuals the model for all inquiry. In the early 1660s, the kings of France and England gave official endorsement to organizations devoted to scientific work, and soon princes all over Europe followed suit. Aristocrats as well as serious experimenters joined these royal societies, and fields as disparate as the design of gardens and the study of populations began to reflect the influence of the scientists.

By the end of the century, especially after the 1687 publication of Newton's masterpiece, which brought the advances in astronomy and physics to a climax, the new provision was in effect. Moreover, the authority now accorded to science gave a final blow to Renaissance assumptions because its achievements provided the decisive argument in the so-called Battle of the Books. With a fierceness that suggested how stubbornly the traditionalists wanted to preserve their beliefs and how urgently the advocates of the new sought to move ahead, a flurry of sharply worded tracts erupted in the late seventeenth and early eighteenth centuries arguing the conflicting merits of the Ancients and the Moderns. At stake was a last desperate attempt by defenders of Renaissance values to argue for the superiority of antiquity. To us, this seems about as arid a dispute as one can imagine, but the earnest pamphlets that it generated reveal the passions of the combatants. For the French, it has remained *the* "querelle" within a long tradition of controversialist literature. A satirist of Jonathan Swift's stature had to come along before anyone could make fun of the entire episode, and the title of his tract gave the episode its English name, the Battle of the Books (fig. 40). Still, one can sympathize with those who saw their most cherished assumptions crumbling around them and remained determined to hang on to their doomed insistence that the ancients knew more than their contemporaries. After Newton, that could no longer be a winning argument, and soon there appeared the first suggestions of the rather different, modern idea of progress: that most areas of human activity and achievement were the beneficiaries of steady and decisive advance.

∽

Among the many signs that the attitudes essential to the Renaissance since its earliest days were passing, one seems particularly ironic, because it reversed the very purpose of the call for a new outlook in the fourteenth century that had set the Renaissance in motion. In a development that would have shocked Petrarch

*Fig. 40 Jonathan Swift's 1697 publication titled* The Battle of the Books *gave its name to the contemporary argument about the relative merits of ancients and moderns. Swift preferred the ancients, and although it was a losing cause, his humor survived: As the frontispiece shows, he saw the fight as a literal battle that took place in a library.*

and his successors, the 1660s and 1670s witnessed a major effort to rehabilitate the Middle Ages. Those who had looked to antiquity for guidance, and had denounced the failures of the intervening centuries, would have been appalled to witness such a revival. Throughout the Renaissance, these in-between years, the "Middle" Ages, had been condemned for their blinkered abandonment of the glorious values of the ancient world. Not only were medieval institutions such as the papacy denounced as corrupt and unworthy but even medieval art, as we have seen, was dismissed as barbaric, or "Gothic." No good word was allowed for the rib vaulting, the flying buttresses, the elaborately carved portals, or the glowing windows that were the culprits responsible for the disappearance of the domes, the curved walls, and the rounded arches of Roman architecture. If popes, cathedrals, and a theology devoted to minutiae had no merit, why should one pay heed to the era that they represented?

Petrarch's rejection of the Middle Ages as a period worthy of study had been upheld by subsequent humanists, from Lorenzo Valla in the fifteenth century to Josef Scaliger in the seventeenth. It was therefore the surest indication that the Renaissance was coming to an end when, between 1667 and 1672, there appeared three volumes of a remarkable work that was a portent of the future. This was the first publication of a redoubtable and influential historian, the French monk Jean Mabillon, and it consisted of a learned and meticulous edition of the works of a famous twelfth-century theologian, St. Bernard of Clairvaux. Over the next few decades, Mabillon, together with colleagues from his order, the Congregation of Saint-Maur, laid down the principles for textual scholarship that have held sway ever since. Adapting the Renaissance insistence on the importance of original documents for the study of the past, he and his colleagues, known as Maurists, began to assemble collections of medieval documents that have remained fundamental to research on the period ever since. Not only did the Maurist publications become models of historical research, but Mabillon himself laid out the basic guidelines for such research, explaining the principles of source criticism and philological analysis in his *De Re Diplo-*

*matica* (1681). The name "diplomatics" has signified the study of medieval texts ever since. All this effort gave the Middle Ages a respectability and an interest that would have been inconceivable in humanist circles during the previous three centuries. It was an unmistakable sign that Renaissance predilections were giving way to new interests.

∾

There was also a vivid indication of shifting values in the visual arts, which again reflected the changed commitments and ambitions of the age. The high emotions of the Baroque gave way to the genteel elegance of Rococo. Where once powerful religious, mythological, and historical dramas were played out on canvas and in stone, there were now sedate pastoral settings, elaborate portraits, and gracefully observed landscapes and representations of daily life. Powerful theatrical scenes and elaborate compositions were replaced by muted emotions and light-hearted decoration (plate 8). Despite occasional exceptions, neither the emulation of antiquity nor religious passion remained as central to artistic expression as they had been throughout the Renaissance.

Much that the Renaissance had brought about was to persist, but the central goals of its culture; the political, social, and economic changes it had brought about; and the set of values it had pursued were all fading into obsolescence during the final decades of the seventeenth century.

∾

In the next chapter we will take a closer look at two of the central processes involved in this change: the new element in attitudes toward war, and the dramatic retreat, in the public sphere, of the belief in the supernatural. If one had to pick two measures of the end of the Renaissance, it would be the erosion of these two ancient assumptions, taken for granted not only during this period but since time immemorial: that war showed man at his finest and most valorous, and that the world could best be understood, and public policy best be determined, through supernatural insight. Put even more strongly, one could argue that the two main forces that dissolved the coherence of the Renaissance were the Thirty Years' War and the Scientific Revolution. It was the revulsion at the former, and the new ways of thinking stimulated by the latter, that sent European society and culture off in new directions. When, as a result, antiwar sentiments finally penetrated the ruling elite, and the rational, mathematical arguments of the scientists triumphed over the reliance on authority or the divine, one could be sure that a new era had come into being.

# Chapter Six

# ART, PROPHECY, AND THE END
# OF THE RENAISSANCE

*T*hus far, we have proceeded in broad strokes. Vast periods, major developments, and shelves of historical interpretations have been encapsulated in a few pages. But we have now reached what, for our purposes, was the most crucial of the transitions from one age to the next. In the story of the march to modernity, the decisive turn, the pivot around which all else revolves, was the long moment (at most half a century long) when the Renaissance came to an end. To flesh out these last days of the period, to give a sense of how so momentous a shift took place, it is necessary to slow down, to look more closely at two of the emblematic developments of these decisive decades.

If a revolution in attitudes toward war and the supernatural—two of the most profound indicators of a culture's values—can stand for the rest of the transformations of the time, we can trace their advance through two types of evidence. By examining these more closely, we will see, first, how artists made antiwar sentiments respectable and heard, even in the elite circles that encompassed the chief warmongers of the age; and second, how the belief in divinely inspired prophecy lost authority in the public sphere, that is, in the eyes of those same elites. On both of these fronts, a new outlook was emerging among the leaders of society that had no precedent in western history.

◈

We have seen that the traditional reliance on prowess in battle as the distinguishing quality of Europe's ruling classes had encountered its first doubts during the Renaissance. Gunpowder had made individual bravado virtually useless, and a new image, emphasizing gentler virtues, had arisen at various Italian courts and had been standardized by Baldassare Castiglione. This did not mean that physical courage became irrelevant to definitions of nobility. It merely paved the way for the new outlook that was to be born amidst the brutality of the Thirty Years' War.

The impact of that drawn-out conflict deserves emphasis. Lest we imagine that it was but one of many wars, and not particularly distinct, we need to recall that, for most Europeans, it represented the extreme case of brutality and violence against which levels of human depravity were judged for generations. The ferocity, callousness, and destructiveness were not equaled again until the Terror in the French Revolution or the World Wars of the twentieth century. When the German general Helmuth von Moltke wanted to suggest what lay ahead as World War I loomed, he predicted (uncannily) that it would be like the Thirty Years' War crammed into four years. It is important, therefore, not to underestimate the trauma that the war caused. As the viciousness of the fighting intensified, alternatives to heroism attracted new attention, and antiwar sentiments for the first time became respectable within Europe's Establishment.

To suggest how revolutionary this transformation was, we can consider one of the most common subjects in European art, the portrait of the prince. The leaders of society had long felt that they were at their most glorious when in military guise, and that was how they had always preferred to be seen. The armed horseman was a favorite pose, derived as it was from the famous Roman statue of Marcus Aurelius. This was the model for dozens of Renaissance portraits, including sculptures by Donatello and Verrocchio (plate 3), and paintings by Uccello and Titian. The most renowned depiction of that devout administrator, the emperor Charles V, was Titian's portrayal that showed him as a Christian knight in full battle gear (plate 4). And there were other ways of emphasizing that a great man's special position derived from his military qualities. Titian put Charles's son, the sober bureaucrat Philip II, in armor as he held up his baby son and celebrated the naval victory of Lepanto. But the equestrian portrait was the favorite, continuing in full vigor through much of the seventeenth century. Then, however, the tradition seemed to lose its forcefulness; by the time of Van Bloemen's *Marlborough and His Officers,* it had become a formality (fig. 41), and even the ever-victorious Napoleon could not restore its allegorical intensity. This loss of conviction in a long-standing genre was one of the casualties of the rethinking of the warrior's virtues that first became fully apparent during the Thirty Years' War.

No artist of the Baroque era conveyed the power and the glory of military accomplishments with more dazzling energy or

*Fig. 41 Pieter van Bloemen's 1714 portrait of the Duke of Marlborough and his officers at Blenheim, a famous victory, indicates how muted the depiction of the military hero had become. No longer particularly splendid, the commander has his presence documented, but he does not even watch the battle behind him.*

greater persuasiveness than Rubens. His gigantic depictions of the rulers of the day, such as Henri IV of France, presented them in full martial triumph. Henri is shown entering Paris as its conqueror, surrounded by glorifications of his victories that merely enhanced his splendor (fig. 42). Even the pacifist James I of England, who was petrified by violence and tried to establish peacemaking as the hallmark of his rule, seemed heroic when he was apotheosized by Rubens on the ceiling of the Banqueting

*Fig. 42    When Rubens in the late 1620s created this enormous canvas of Henri IV entering Paris, his subject had been dead nearly twenty years. But the triumphalism and military valor remained central to the image of the king.*

House in London (fig. 43). That was still the way kings had to look when on their way to heaven. And Rubens also exalted military valor in other ways—for example, in a rousing series of paintings celebrating the life of the Roman consul, Decius Mus, who had given his life so that his army could win a crucial battle (fig. 44). But in the 1620s, as the Thirty Years' War began to spread a destructiveness never before seen in central Europe, he began to convey different values.

It has been argued that Rubens's thoughts turned to peace partly because he had served as a diplomat for the Habsburgs, and also because peace in his eyes meant the achievement of hegemony by his Spanish masters. Neither influence, however, can have generated the real antipathy to armed conflict that now surfaced in his work; it cannot be interpreted as just another means of advancing his patrons' interests. Far more

*Fig. 43  Rubens's* Apotheosis of James I *was installed in the ceiling of the Banqueting House in London in 1636. The depiction of the king in this heroic fashion indicates how important such imagery was, even for a ruler whose reputation was decidedly unheroic and who saw himself as a dedicated pacifist.*

plausible as a motive was his abhorrence for the violence, intensifying all around him, that he was to deplore in a famous letter. For accounts such as the following were common in the pamphlets and newspapers of the day:

*Fig. 44   The story of the Roman general Decius Mus, who dreamed on the eve of a battle that the leader of the victorious army would be killed, and then deliberately put himself in harm's way, was emblematic of the cult of heroism. Rubens's eight-canvas depiction of Decius Mus's life (here he tells his troops of his dream) was painted in 1616–1617, on the eve of the Thirty Years' War that was to change Rubens's view of warfare.*

Wallenstein's troops . . . had prepared axes, hammers, and cudgels for their plundering, and they used them as butchers use instruments when slaughtering cattle. They split open peoples' heads, threw them to the ground, stamped on them and crushed them with their feet so that the blood spurted forth not only from open wounds but also from necks, ears, and noses. It is generally agreed that of the hundreds of citizens the troops encountered not one escaped unharmed.

Rubens's response was not an abstract endorsement of peace, nor political propaganda, but a deeply felt personal engagement, as one can see in his first major treatment of the issue, his *Peace and War* or, more precisely, *Minerva Protects Pax from Mars* (plate 6). For Rubens, this standard mythological subject was the opportunity for a powerful statement. Mars's realm is not a neutral background, as normally shown, but a dark land of destructive Furies that contrasts sharply (as the god himself seems to acknowledge, in his surprised backward glance) with the life-giving kingdom of Peace. To drive the point home, moreover, Rubens portrayed, as the beneficiaries of peace—the characters for whom the entire scene is played—the three children of his friend and host in England, Balthasar Gerbier. This was no tale from Olympus but a direct comment on the times and the prospects of its younger generation. And Rubens made the connection explicit a few years later in a moving letter describing his painting *The Horrors of War* (fig. 45). After explicating the classical references and symbols in detail, he continues:

> The mother with a child in her arms indicates that fecundity . . . and charity are thwarted by War, which corrupts and destroys everything. . . . That grief-stricken woman clothed in black . . . is the unfortunate Europe, who for so many years now has suffered plunder, outrage, and misery, which are so injurious to everyone it is unnecessary to go into detail.

*Fig. 45   By 1637, Rubens was painting an openly antiwar scene,* The Horrors of War. *The message, as he described it in a famous letter, is unmistakable. The redeeming virtues, the noble qualities, have gone; horror remains.*

The imagery is classical, but the subject is the modern world.

Nor did Rubens hesitate to make the point openly, even to a Habsburg hero whom he also portrayed in the standard equestrian pose of military glory: the Infante Ferdinand, brother of the king of Spain and the victor of Nördlingen, one of the decisive battles of the Thirty Years' War. When Ferdinand was appointed governor of the Netherlands and made his official entry into Rubens's home city of Antwerp, the artist supervised and designed the decorations that greeted the new ruler as he progressed through the streets. The climax was reached when the procession arrived at a huge representation of the Temple of Janus. Roman tradition held that Mars rushed forth to do battle through the temple's open doors (also visible in

*Fig. 46 The 1635 entry of Archduke Ferdinand into Antwerp was cele-
brated by decorations and temporary archways designed by Rubens. This
1641 engraving of one of the scenes is notable for its emphasis on the quest for
peace amidst the Thirty Years' War of Ferdinand's predecessor, Isabella (in a
nun's habit).*

*The Horrors of War*), which remained closed in peacetime. The
decorations have long vanished, but because Rubens's designs
were engraved and published after his death, we can tell what
message they conveyed. On the left of the temple stood person-
ifications of violence and its effects, including Discord. To the
right stood the results of Peace: Abundance and Tranquillity.
But it is the central section, the scene at the doors themselves,
that is of special interest (fig. 46). As the Furies hold open the

portal for the blind rage of Mars, Peace seeks to close it, all the while looking sadly at her audience, presumably Ferdinand himself. What is most significant, though, is the figure in the habit of a nun directly behind her: a portrait of Ferdinand's predecessor, his aunt, Isabella, who had worked for peace and now appropriately tried to push the door shut. It is a direct appeal to the new governor for an end to the fighting.

Thus did Rubens, reacting to the destruction all around him, feel compelled to tell his patrons—heroes and promoters of war though they might be—that valor was a limited virtue. He was no mordant outsider like Pieter Brueghel, who had heaped scorn on bellicosity, cruelty, and oppression from the vantage point of the victim; rather, and perhaps more remarkably, Rubens was closely associated with members of the very Establishment that perpetrated atrocities in the name of religion or military ideals. He was calling eloquently for new values, and doing so from within. Not surprisingly, Rubens in his last years turned away from heroism and produced instead a series of glowing landscapes that were hymns to nature; in these paintings, human beings were relegated to incidental roles.

The first sign of change in Rubens's outlook, *Peace and War,* had begun to take shape, appropriately, during his visit to England in 1629 and 1630 (plate 6). For it was in London that he had encountered a royal court, Charles I's, that had managed to stay out of the worst of the Thirty Years' War and indeed was proclaiming its commitment to peace as its distinctive quality. Rubens acknowledged this unusual preference by portraying the king as St. George, not killing the dragon, but swordless and returning the bands of her dress (with which he had bound the monster) to the princess—that is, to his queen, Henrietta Maria, the favorite personification of peace in the imagery of the Caroline court. The cynical might say that Charles, penurious and outgunned, had no choice but to cultivate ideals different from most monarchs because he was incapable of waging war. But his father was a genuine pacifist, and it seems clear that the palace of Whitehall in the 1620s and 1630s was a crucial center of the shift in sensibilities that occurred in these decades.

Charles still appeared as the traditional armored knight on horseback in more than one portrait by his chief painter, van Dyck. But he also encouraged the more domestic qualities that went along with a peace-loving image. The Dutch artist Mytens depicted him and the queen showered with flowers as they set off on their beloved sport of hunting. And the lowering of the heroic pitch is also apparent in van Dyck's most famous portrait, traditionally called *Charles I at the Hunt* (plate 7). The king is no longer on the great horse; the walking stick has replaced the commander's baton; all is calm and pastoral; and the setting is perhaps best described by a stage instruction for one of the masques that served as the court's chief medium for the praise of peace. The Furies having been displaced, the scene change calls for

> a calm, the sky serene, afar off Zephyrs appeared breathing a gentle gale: in the landscape were corn fields and pleasant trees, sustaining vines fraught with grapes, and in some of the furthest parts villages, with all such things as might express a country in peace, rich and fruitful.

So enamored were the royal couple with such evocations of tranquility that they had themselves painted twice, by Mytens and van Dyck, in a pose symbolizing their rejection of

*Fig. 47    Of the many depictions of Charles I and Henrietta Maria that van Dyck painted, this double portrait of 1632 most clearly highlights the wish for peace that the queen, in particular, represented.*

war (fig. 47). Charles hands the queen the laurel wreath of the victor, and seeks from her the olive, symbol of reconciliation, all the while holding his sword firmly in its scabbard. When the baby Prince of Wales enlarged the family, in a portrait by Pot, they sat with their regalia in a room littered with the olive leaves of peace.

Across the North Sea, although they were fighting for their very existence as a nation, the Dutch, too, reacted against the Thirty Years' War with demands for different values. This was a less aristocratic society, but still the ruling House of Orange, despite opposition from the merchants of Amsterdam, could confidently assert that war was essential. In response, there appeared the unusual image of the sleeping Mars. Its most popular exemplar was a striking engraving

*Fig. 48   This engraving by the Dutch artist Jacques de Gheyn was produced in the first years of the Thirty Years' War, possibly even before the Dutch entered the conflict in 1621, and uses an image of Mars asleep as a plea for peace.*

produced around 1620 by the well-known artist Jacques de Gheyn (fig. 48). In case the symbolic message might not be self-explanatory, the caption left no doubt: "Mars rests after crowning himself with glory; may he rest more gloriously from now on for the good of the people." And the theme was taken up a few years later in a painting of a sleeping man in armor by Terbrugghen (fig. 49). Here the point was made explicit by a rosette built into the breastplate that showed the lion known as Leo Belgicus, the standard symbol of the Netherlands. Like de Gheyn, Terbrugghen hoped that the Dutch Mars would sleep for the good of his people. It is a powerful image, but also a highly unorthodox use of the Roman god: to raise questions about the virtue of war. And its very rarity suggests,

*Fig. 49   It is quite possible that Hendrick Terbrugghen saw the engraving by his fellow Dutchman de Gheyn (fig. 48) before painting this* Sleeping Mars. *Especially suggestive is the fact that the Belgian Lion, the symbol of the Netherlands, appears in the rosette on the breastplate.*

when it crops up unexpectedly in the work of the principal court painter of Spain, that it found an echo even among the enemies of the Dutch.

Whether or not Velázquez had seen the de Gheyn engraving, it seems remarkable that just a few years later (in 1640) he too should have shown Mars in so unlikely a pose: pensive,

*Fig. 50 Velázquez's image of Mars, though painted in 1640 for a royal hunting lodge, might well owe its notion of a weary god of war to the theme de Gheyn and Terbrugghen had earlier explored (figs. 48 and 49). It certainly dates from a time when the strains of the Thirty Years' War were seriously affecting Spain.*

disconsolate, his armor cast aside (fig. 50). It is true that this was a painting for a hunting lodge—not a place for serious statements—and that it could well have referred to Lucian's witty dialogue about Mars's troubles with Venus. But its resigned and somewhat melancholy, brooding air hardly suggests frivolity (not exactly Velázquez's forte anyway), and there is no obvious link with the Greek tale. Yet it is above all the painting's recollection of the earlier, and similarly unconventional, treatments of Mars, its reflection of the shift in attitudes that was so vivid elsewhere in the art of the 1630s, and its accord with the

*Fig. 51* The Surrender of Breda, *painted by Velázquez in 1635 for a royal Hall of Realms that commemorated Spain's victories, shows in the central figure of Spinola, the Spanish general who is comforting his vanquished foe, that war is not merely a matter of triumph and valor but also a time for magnanimity and compassion. There may also be a hint here that Velázquez knew Spinola had been a strong advocate of peace.*

outlook of a previous masterpiece by Velázquez that lends credence to the view that this was not solely a decorative work but another reflection of the changing values of the age.

The previous masterpiece is the celebrated scene from the Dutch war, *The Surrender of Breda* (fig. 51). Created in 1635 for the Hall of Realms in the king's new palace in Madrid, it

*Fig. 52 Mayno's* Recapture of Bahia, *also painted in 1635 for the Hall of Realms, emphasizes the charity and grief that accompany war; the work adds further dimensions to the compassion one sees in the* Breda *that hung nearby (fig. 51).*

joined a roomful of glorifications of the Habsburgs. Celebrations of victories on palatial walls were a traditional means of self-advertisement. But the Velázquez *Breda* was very different, as was another picture in that same hall, Mayno's *Recapture of Bahia* (fig. 52).

What was remarkable about both paintings, especially in that location, was not merely that they refused to proclaim unabashedly the majesty of war but that they emphasized quite different virtues even as they commemorated Habsburg victories. Equally extraordinary was their resolve (as with Rubens in his *Peace and War*) to achieve their impact by means that are direct and recognizable, and not through generalized abstractions. It is this personal association, this reference to the familiar, that argues most cogently for the strength of feeling we can perceive behind the changing outlook of the period. For in Mayno's *Bahia* the king himself, his minister Olivares, and his commander don Fadrique look at the scene in the foreground, where the distress and the charity that war can inspire receive the focus of attention. Perhaps the invocation of humble Christian virtues was appropriate to a friar such as Mayno, but their forceful expression in this setting remains remarkable. So is the emphasis on compassion that animates Velázquez's *Breda,* and especially its central figure, Spinola, the great general who was known to have urged an end to Spain's debilitating wars. Like other pictures in the hall, the *Breda* gives little sign of the exultation of victory. Instead of delight at the successes of Habsburg arms, it shows us figures who are as pensive (not unlike Velázquez's *Mars*) on the Spanish as on the Dutch side. And the central gesture is an act of comforting magnanimity, not triumph, by Spinola. Despite the purpose for which these works were produced, commissioned as they were by a king constantly at war, they made no case for heroism or valor. Rather, in accordance with the new mood of the 1630s, they extolled other sources of virtue for the Crown of Spain.

A final set of evidence comes from France and indicates the lasting consequences of the shifting viewpoints of the 1620s and 1630s. This story begins with Jacques Callot, the master engraver who, in addition to illustrating festivals, buildings, and other standard scenes, served his patrons by filling requests for vast birds'-eye views of important battles. Their scale is huge, commensurate with the subject matter, and they required multiple plates. In a more precise documentary recreation than Velázquez attempted, Callot recorded the capture of Breda in a vast engraving of 1630; and he did the same, also in 1630, for the French king's capture of the Huguenot strongholds at La Rochelle and the Isle of Ré. But then came the remarkable change of heart.

From his home in Lorraine and his travels in the Netherlands, Callot had firsthand knowledge of the fighting of the Thirty Years' War and its effects, and he drew on his experiences for his last major work, the series of etchings published in 1633 as *The Miseries of War.* These small pictures, easily transportable and widely known, exposed in realistic detail the day-to-day consequences of military affairs. Their bitter social commentary—as unexpected, given Callot's previous work, as Rubens's conversion—has inspired antiwar pictures ever since. They tell a story that begins with recruitment and a battle and ends with an ironic distribution of rewards. But the message of their fourteen central scenes is unmistakable: Pillage, plunder, and destruction are the inevitable adjuncts of war. Soldiers, one caption tells us, "ravage everywhere. Nothing escapes their hands. . . . All with one accord viciously commit theft, kidnapping, murder and rape." There is no glory; only loss, vengeance, and mutilation, the crippled and the dead.

The most famous etching, *The Hanging,* takes the implications one step further (fig. 53). The executed figures in *The Hanging*—"these infamous and abandoned thieves," as the caption puts it—are themselves victims of war, as their crutches, in a pile below the tree, attest. And the priest on the ladder who holds the cross up to them may even be taken to

*Fig. 53   Jacques Callot's series of engravings* The Miseries of War
*(1633) give away their purpose in their title. This is the most famous
image, the hanging of plundering soldiers, though their crutches suggest that
they, too, are casualties of war. And one wonders whether the priest's blessing
is intended as an irony in this war of religion.*

represent the religious zeal that has fueled the violence. In his
preliminary drawing for the scene, moreover, Callot made the
connection between sacrifice, war, and religion almost explicit.
Here the tree itself is a cross.

Yet the shift in representations of war did not consist merely
of a new willingness to question the virtues of heroism and propose alternative values. It led also to a devaluation of the military
as a symbol for larger meanings. This draining away of the allegorical and moral implications of battle was as profound a reversal as the surge in the criticisms of war by Establishment
artists. The first widespread examples come from the Dutch,
who perhaps were so used to war that they could reduce its
scenes to one among the many unglamorous features of daily
life that populate their art. In fact, the ordinariness of the soldier
and his activities became something of a genre, practiced by

*Fig. 54    Gerard Terborch's* Officer Writing a Letter, *painted in the late 1650s, shows how prosaic, almost domestic, scenes with soldiers had become. The trumpeter who is to deliver the letter even seems to eye us knowingly, as if the letter were pursuing something other than military business.*

painters who specialized in the subject just as others devoted themselves to skaters or taverns. The earliest master of the theme, William Duyster, who died in 1635, particularly liked guard rooms; here, armed men lead lives as prosaic and familiar as those seen in any domestic interior. They sleep, smoke, and suffer endless boredom as they pursue a commonplace occupation. His younger and more talented contemporary, Gerard Terborch, used the genre as one unremarkable aspect of his many-sided explorations of domestic space (fig. 54).

Another new genre that had a similar effect was the so-called Battle Without a Hero. The notion that one could portray an engagement without defining the participants was the very

*Fig. 55    Philips Wouwerman's* Assault on a Bridge, *dating from around the end of the Thirty Years' War, is full of the fire and drama of combat, but, like the hundreds of other battle scenes he painted, it lacks heroes and gives no hint of the valor that once was the mark of the warrior.*

antithesis of previous assumptions. If there was no paragon to glorify, or even the army of a specific combatant to honor, nobody benefited. Such paintings turned combat into an event that, if not quite mundane, was nevertheless not marked by special virtue or renown. An early example, appropriately, was one of the etchings in Callot's *Miseries*. But it was again a Dutchman who made the subject his own: Philips Wouwerman. Wouwerman, active from the 1640s, was staggeringly prolific, with perhaps a thousand paintings or more to his name (fig. 55). He doubtless repeated what sold well, which means that his battle scenes, produced by the dozen, were prized because they were neutral: almost decorative, nonpreachy representations of a part of life. Even the fighting itself, though occasionally brutal, is treated primarily as an occasion for the documentary recording of a recognizable phenomenon. Full of action and movement it may be, but it is certainly not magnificent.

The results of this broad-gauged reorientation reached even into the portrayal of bellicose kings at war. When Claude showed Louis XIII at the siege of La Rochelle (a military event that the monarch in fact attended for several months) the occasion is more social than glorious. Callot's antiheroic stance in the *Miseries* has here reached into the highest levels of court patronage. For Claude, also from Lorraine, made a copy of Callot's etchings, and he undoubtedly felt an affinity for the lessons they conveyed. It is true that his aesthetic inclinations tended toward the pastoral; he was not likely to infuse a battle scene with powerful Rubensian drama. But the bucolic restraint of *The Siege of La Rochelle by Louis XIII* is still a remarkable indication of the changing values of the time.

The best testimony to their lasting impact is their persistence even into the glory-seeking reign of Louis XIII's son, Louis XIV. Wars continued, of course, and despite the effort after Westphalia to make them less passionate and bloody, they remained sources of fame and honor for their leaders. But the connection was no longer unequivocal. Alternative founts of virtue and superiority had appeared—for Louis they included an association with the life-giving sun and, in a famous portrait, with overwhelming richness and elegance. Moreover, battle pictures had taken on a documentary character that lessened their allegorical value. The heroic imagery did not vanish, but its force was declining—which helps account for the extraordinary decision to re-carve Bernini's triumphant equestrian statue of the king "in the attitude of majesty and command" (to quote the sculptor himself) into a portrait of an ancient warrior, Marcus Curtius. That Bernini's masterpiece should have encountered such a reaction when it arrived in France suggests how far style, taste, and the status of the warrior had altered, even under a militant and self-aggrandizing regime. Broadening the context, one might even claim that the rejection Bernini was a telling indication that the Renaissance was over.

The chief recorder of battles for Louis XIV was a Fleming, Adam Frans van der Meulen (fig. 56). As one account of his work notes, he had "a talent for the elegant painting of colorful military scenes. The true brutality of the events is hidden behind a pall of gunpowder smoke in the distance, and attention is drawn away from it by the handsomely dressed cavalry officers in the foreground." From time to time, the officers include the king himself, but the atmosphere remains the same, as it does in the occasional rendition of such subjects by Louis's chief court painter, Charles Le Brun. Here qualities of grace and social refinement replace the thunder and the glory. A drawing by Le Brun of the king at a siege makes warfare almost a domestic event: The king is accompanied by the queen and her ladies as a group of burghers surrender their city. There is no place in such company for assertions of grandeur or bravery.

Perhaps the most remarkable example from Louis's reign of the influence of the revolution in values in the 1620s and 1630s is a painting by Le Brun that commemorates France's declaration of war on the Netherlands in 1672 (fig. 57). Commissioned to celebrate a momentous royal decision, the artist

*Fig. 56    Van der Meulen's depiction of a minor battle near Mont Cassel in 1677 is typical of the many occasions when he showed Louis XIV, almost invisible in the foreground, amidst war. The topography, not to mention the artful tree, seem almost more important than either king or battle. Thus had the valor of war ceased to be central to ideals of nobility.*

does not simply extol (as he might well have done) the valorous ambitions of a dynamic king. Instead, he bluntly raises the dilemma about the nature of war that the generation of Rubens and Callot had posed some forty years earlier. On the right,

*Fig. 57   Painted in 1671, on the eve of Louis XIV's invasion of the Nether-lands, Le Brun's* Decision for War *offers two strongly contrasting images of the consequences of plunging into battle.*

Mars promises the laurel wreath of victory to the enthroned monarch; but on the left Peace and Minerva, the goddess of wisdom, point to a scene of the horrors of war, laced with thunder and lightning, that echoes Rubens's version of the subject (fig. 45). That both sides of the issue—without a clear preference for either, despite Le Brun's knowledge of the outcome—could be presented so forcefully to a belligerent king who was already committed to battle indicates how far the transformation of sensibilities had advanced since Rubens emblazoned Henri IV's entry into Paris half a century before (fig. 42).

Naturally, the fighting and the identification of virtue with victory did not cease. Far from it. And even individuals were not of single minds. Rubens continued to produce heroic portraits and martial artifacts long after his *Peace and War*. Nor did Velázquez stop conveying the power of the Habsburgs just because he had completed his *Breda,* though in his last years he did concentrate increasingly on domestic scenes at the Spanish court. Fundamental transitions take time, and this one was no exception. But there can be little doubt that the less ideological age of the late seventeenth and eighteenth centuries treated warfare and its meaning in a much more realistic, nuanced, and balanced fashion. When deep passions once again animated combat, as they did after 1789, glory and brutality could again contend for recognition as the dominant image of war—David vs. Goya, to personify the issue. That such a controversy could arise at all, however, was due in the first instance to the crucial achievement of those who had redefined the values associated with the battlefield during the generation of the Thirty Years' War, and particularly its artists. In the images through which this increasingly genteel society saw itself, they had made an antiwar position respectable, they had desymbolized the battlefield, and they had validated alternatives to valor as the distinguishing mark of the gentleman. Whether they were a vanguard, or merely the instrument through which a broader unease was expressed, the message they conveyed was unequivocal. It was no longer just the caustic outsider, the critic of society, but the Establishment itself that resonated to Milton's troubling question: "What can war but endless war still breed?"

⟨✦⟩

Where the supernatural is concerned, we need to begin with an event whose full meaning will have to be teased out by looking backward as well as forward. It is an episode that embodied the age that was dying even as it heralded a different future. At issue was Oliver Cromwell's effort to re-admit Jews to England some 350 years after they had been expelled.

To understand that effort, we have to understand how deeply the Bible had permeated, not only Cromwell's consciousness (as we have already observed in his reference to Jericho), but also the assumptions of most of his contemporaries. They would certainly have heard the echo of its language, and applauded the sentiments, when he sent his report of his victory at Preston to the Speaker of the House of Commons: "Surely, Sir, this is nothing but the hand of God; and whenever anything in this world is exalted, or exalts itself, God will pull it down; for this is the day wherein He alone will be exalted." It is in this context of a pervasive reliance on biblical reference that we need to see his initiative to bring the Jews back to England.

There are other ways to interpret the story. Some scholars have noted the emphasis on the economic benefits of a Jewish trading community that marked the written appeal for the readmission that was submitted to Cromwell by an Amsterdam rabbi, Menasseh ben Israel. But there is little indication that such "modern" arguments carried any weight with Cromwell and his colleagues. They relied, instead, on other forms of justification, as is apparent from the central event in the process: the "conference concerning the Jews" that convened "in a withdrawing-room in Whitehall" on December 12, 1655, in the presence of Oliver Cromwell and leading figures from England's judiciary and clergy. This was the decisive moment in the entire affair, and we need to take note of the concerns that, according to contemporaries, entered into the deliberations. The economic argument that Menasseh ben Israel had made on behalf of his co-religionists attracted the attention only of a few London businessmen, and indeed was counterproductive because they feared the competition that might ensue. The focus of the discussions was, rather, the philosophic, legal, and religious considerations that the issue raised. These all seem to have been relatively straightforward, except for one.

As a contemporary observer put it, the assembly met to advise Cromwell "by reason, Law-learning, Scripture-prophecy, and every source of light for the human mind." That was a tall order, but one standard stands out from the rest. We may have a good idea as to the products of reason, law, and general enlightenment, but what was the meaning, in this context, of "Scripture-prophecy"? Its inclusion as a major preoccupation of the conferees in Whitehall hints unmistakably at an aspect of the Renaissance mentality that would not long outlive the mid-seventeenth century.

What was meant by "Scripture-prophecy"? Precisely because it seems so unfamiliar (at least as a consideration in public policy) in this day and age, we need to experience more closely, in all its richness, the flavor of this basic interest of Renaissance thought. By so doing, we will put the events of December 1655 in context, and thus be able to gauge the immensity of the change that was about to take place.

One way to get a feel for this concern is to plunge into a characteristic example of the genre, and we might start with one that was published in 1621, not by some wild-eyed divine but by a distinguished representative of England's Establishment, Sir Henry Finch. An eminently respectable lawyer and member of Parliament, Finch was part of the elite segment of his profession known as serjeants-at-law. He was also one of a small coterie of learned jurists whom the Chancellor of England assembled to try to codify the Statutes of the Realm. This was the solid and sober gentleman, knighted for his services to the law, who published a book, 235 pages long, that sought to elucidate the major prophetic texts of the Bible. And he had a field day with one of the most famous of those texts, the seventh chapter of the book of Daniel. His commentary on just one phrase in that chapter is as good a way as any to suggest the tone and purpose of the Scripture-prophecy of his time.

In the space of twenty-eight verses, Daniel recounted a dream of four beasts, representing four successive kingdoms over the earth. The last beast, he said, had ten horns, all of which were kings in turn; they finally gave way, however, to just one, who ruled, according to verse twenty-five, until "a time and times and the dividing of time," at which point the kingdom of the saints would finally arise. According to many interpreters, this fourth beast was Rome, or its successor, the Holy Roman Empire. The horns, or kingdoms, were the various states that had arisen during the previous thousand years. These had come and gone, and therefore the contemporary world was about to enter the final age. Finch, however, was more explicit. The last horn, or kingdom, he said, represented the Turk (the Ottoman Empire ruled from Constantinople), and in his view "the continuance of the Turkish tyranny"—that is, the number of years it would endure—could be worked out with the help of the phrase from verse twenty-five ("a time and times and the dividing of time"), which he slightly amended to "its tyranny should be a time, times, and a division of times."

But what did that mean, specifically? To Finch, it was quite simple. The Turkish tyranny had begun, so everyone agreed, in or about the year 1300. Finch thought the biblical phrase "a time" had to be a round number—that is, 100 years. The next biblical word, "times" in the plural, had to be double the word "time" in the singular—that is, 200 years. Naturally, therefore, the phrase "a dividing of time" had to be half of "time"—that is, 50 years. Using straightforward addition, the three numbers of "a time, times, and a dividing of time" totaled 350; thus the Turkish tyranny would come to an end 350 years after its start in 1300: in other words, in the year 1650.

As it happens, we can find, in one seventeenth-century tract or another, a prophecy of the second coming, the end of the world, the arrival of the Messiah, or the Day of Judgment for every year from 1650 to 1666. The latter was particularly common, because the most quoted verse in another favorite prophetic book, Revelations, came from the end of Chapter 13: "Here is wisdom. Let him that hath understanding count the number of the beast; for it is the number of a man; and his number is six hundred threescore and six." To the number 666, it seemed almost self-evident to add a thousand, and thus to find the relevant year, 1666.

Few of the authors of these tracts had the standing or the worldly success that Finch enjoyed. But many were eminently respectable, even if their contemporaries were not always convinced about their sanity or their willingness to abide by social norms, let alone their religious or political orthodoxy. Dame Eleanor Davies, for example, widely known as Lady Eleanor, who published more than seventy prophetic tracts between 1625 and 1652, was the sister of an earl and thus sprang from the upper reaches of the English aristocracy. Like Finch, she had a fondness for numbers—for her it was 25, because that was the day of the month the Virgin gave birth, the year in his life and in the century when Charles I ascended the throne, the year when Lady Eleanor began having her visions, and a convenient multiple for forecasting the end of days. She landed repeatedly in prison—among her faux pas was predicting, accurately, the assassination of a royal minister, the Duke of Buckingham—and it is hardly surprising that one of her critics used her own fondness for anagrams (her maiden name, Eleanor Audelie, became Reveale O Daniel) against her by turning Dame Eleanor Davies into Never So Mad a Ladie. But, for all the doubts about her sanity, and the irritations caused by her many unpopular or impolitic prophecies, she always received the deference that was considered appropriate to her aristocratic rank.

Still, it was not Davies's and Finch's status that explains the interest or fear they aroused. In this field of endeavor, in fact, their social position was exceptional. Nevertheless, although most of their fellow prophets lacked their rank in society, many did attract just as much attention. And there were scores of them, proclaiming their visions in every area of Europe. Whether they put their revelations into print or left a record only because they came under the scrutiny of officialdom, they seem consistently to have been remarkable characters, capable of stimulating strong emotions. Examples include the Welshman Arise Evans, who appeared at Charles I's court at Greenwich and tactfully thundered out promises of the king's imminent death; the Castilian Lucrecia de Leon, who foretold the defeat of the Spanish Armada a year before it set sail; and the trio of Bohemians, including Christoph Kotter and Nicholas Drabik (two colleagues of the famous scholar Jan Amos Comenius), who explained that 1666, the Year of the Beast, would see the collapse of the Roman Church.

Their presence in all regions of Europe, their tendency to get into trouble with the authorities, and their occasional international reputations testify to the importance of the phenomenon they represented in the culture of the age. It would have surprised no one, for example, that Kotter's and Drabik's prophecies were translated into English and published in London. But why?

It is true that, from time to time, such prophecies proved to be uncannily correct. Lucrecia's vision of the defeat of the Armada was dismayingly accurate; so too was Lady Eleanor's prediction of Buckingham's death. But the failures vastly outnumbered the triumphs, and it was clearly not the expectation of precise forecasting that drew people to the prophets. The Quaker visionary James Nayler, for example, published forty-four prophetic tracts in little more than ten years; but what inspired his audience (and troubled the authorities) was not so much the specifics of what he said as the mesmerizing effect he had on those who heard him. When he preached, soon after a military engagement in 1650, an army officer said: "I was struck with more terror by the preaching of James Nayler than I was at the battle of Dunbar." What we need to understand, therefore, is not charisma itself; that has its power in every generation. Rather, we have to appreciate why the fire and brimstone, the mystical and apocalyptic content of the message, were so appealing: why they were taken seriously even by Cromwell's Council in 1655, not because of some detailed prediction, but because prophecy itself—whether issuing from a cleric or from an inspired soul—had a special standing in this world.

Foretelling the future had been a continuing tradition in the West at least since the times of Moses and Deborah, of the Sybils and the Delphic Oracle. Famous in the late Middle Ages had been the Italian abbot Joachim of Fiore and the Swedish founder of a new order of nuns, St. Birgitta. And the Renaissance had witnessed the appearance of many charismatic preachers, not to mention waves of mystic fervor. The fiery Dominican Girolamo Savonarola had Florence, the most sophisticated and materialistic city of Europe, in his thrall for four years in the 1490s. The more he proclaimed his messages of doom, of the imminence of plague and destruction, the more captivated the Florentines became. Forty years later, Michelangelo told a friend that he could still hear Savonarola's voice ringing in his ears.

These episodes, however, were all transitory. A prophet or a mystic caused a sensation and then faded from view. Thus, by the time Savonarola announced that his message would live on long after his execution, the very people whom he had persuaded to burn their vanities were already back in the market for jewelry and art. Somewhere in the mid-sixteenth century, however, as the sense of crisis quickened, the pattern began to change. The prophets and mystics multiplied, and their impact became more sustained.

Just four years after Martin Luther began his protest in 1517, for example, three laymen from the nearby town of Zwickau appeared in his home town, Wittenberg. Taken seriously by some of Luther's colleagues, they asked for endorsement of the messages they were receiving directly from God. But Luther would have none of it. He denounced them, and preached eight sermons about the dangers of prophecy. Such attempts to repress the call of the spirit, however, were to no avail. For the next century, the obsession with the truth of God's word that led, on the one hand, to intolerance, religious war, and persecution, led on the other to an anxious searching for heavenly revelation. This was the great age of Spanish mysticism, of wandering prophets in central Europe, and of millenarian sects everywhere.

These outpourings, moreover, were only one symptom of a much broader resort to otherworldly speculations and desperate quests for reassurance amidst the upheavals and troubles of the age. Building on assumptions that were centuries old, Europe entered a golden age of prophecy, speculation, and also (not unrelated) the most intense witchcraft hysteria it had ever seen. The followers of prophets did not cause high drama to match the hunting of witches, but the yearning for simple, supernatural explanations amidst an age of social and religious turmoil was much the same whether the subject was danger from a witch or messages from the Almighty. It was no surprise that, in seventeenth-century London, a substantial body of citizens became convinced "that in Suffolk there is a prophet raised up to come and preach the Everlasting Gospel to them, and he stays but for a vocal call from Heaven to send him, which is expected daily."

This was another variation on the mystical and messianic promises that were so common at the time. Nobody had actually appeared yet, but already the prophet was expected to be marked specifically by "a vocal call from Heaven." No wonder dreamers came forward to claim the prize, in Suffolk and elsewhere. For in this case a very particular prophecy was called for. The "Everlasting Gospel" mentioned in the report referred to a prophecy of Joachim of Fiore, which divided history, not into Daniel's four kingdoms, with a fifth monarchy heralding the millennium, but rather into three ages. The first, of the Father and the Old Testament, was a time of fear before Christ's birth; the second, of the Son and the New Testament, was the current age of faith; and the third, of the Holy Ghost and the Everlasting Gospel, was soon to arrive and bring eternal love and liberty to all men. One can well understand how appealing that vision must have been to a people wracked by confessional struggle and the vicious persecutions that marked Europe's religious wars.

Yet those who longed to comprehend the world or know the future did not confine themselves to the insights offered by religion—whether positive, in the case of prophecy, or negative, when derived from witchcraft. For this was also the golden century of astrology, another fount of prediction with origins that lay deep in antiquity. Among the upper classes throughout Europe at this time, a consultation with an astrologer was the height of respectability. He offered reassurance and explanation to the troubled, and he was a fashionable and sought-after figure. The most successful not only moved in the highest social circles but also earned small fortunes.

The convergence of astrology with messianism and prophecy is most clearly reflected in the reaction to two eclipses of the sun that occurred in the 1650s. The first, "Black Monday," March 29, 1652, lasted for longer than two hours from start to finish in much of western Europe, and included in Paris and London five sixths of a total eclipse. The second, on August 12, 1654, was slightly briefer and reached only two thirds of totality. Both, however, became occasions for foreboding and astrological prophecy.

For reasons that are still unclear, the first eclipse became a cause célèbre only in England, the second only on the Continent. But the fuss was extraordinary. In 1652, people fled from London and bought elixirs from charlatans; and in 1654, the French were convinced they had to stay indoors, spread perfume about, and keep their houses dark. In The Hague, according to one account, the anticipation caused "such prodigious fear among many people that they want to flee the world itself." There were similar concerns in central Europe, in Poland, and in Sweden. Everywhere, thanks to the foreknowledge of the eclipses, astrologers had a field day. One "Scripture-prophet" said that the 1652 conjunction heralded the rise of the Fifth Monarchy. Two dozen or more publications on the subject appeared in England—during the crucial month of March 1652, it seems to have been the focus of more than a quarter of the tracts coming off the presses—and on the Continent two years later the eclipse inspired at least sixty pamphlets or books. Literacy at this time had reached only about a third of a city's population (and less in the countryside), but it was common among the elite; the popularity of these works is thus a telling indication that the belief in prophecy pervaded the leaders of society as well as those below them in rank, whom we might otherwise assume to have been more credulous.

What is most instructive about the orgy of print and comment is its sheer volume, consisting as it did of countless stories in that new form of publication, the newspaper, as well as hundreds, or perhaps thousands, of sermons, of which only a handful were published, though one can imagine the multitudes who heard them preached. After all, solar eclipses are common events. They occur roughly every eighteen months, and although they are restricted to only part of the earth, most areas experience at least two every decade. And even partial eclipses, taking place behind cloud cover, have visible effects. By the period we are speaking of, moreover, they were already receiving systematic attention and objective explanation from the new breed of astronomers, armed with telescopes. One of the most famous, Johannes Kepler, had compared and analyzed the forty-six lunar eclipses that had taken place between 1572 and

1625; another, the Frenchman Pierre Gassendi, wrote a little book to denounce what he considered the nonsense spawned by the 1654 eclipse.

There had been nothing like this outburst before, even though Kepler himself had been a noted astrologer, and there had been celestial events far more unusual than eclipses—the appearance of new stars in 1572 and 1604 and of comets in 1580 and 1618. The growing rationalization and secularization of nature by the ever more prominent scientists of the time seemed to have begun to subdue the promises of upheaval that were prompted by eclipses—that is, until the 1650s.

The efflorescence of dire predictions in 1652 and 1654 was undoubtedly stimulated by the contemporary openness to apocalyptic passions. The most notorious of the commentaries on the 1654 eclipse made the link directly. Because 1,656 years had elapsed between the Creation and Noah's flood, the author argued, one could expect a new flood (this time of fire, not water) 1,656 years after the birth of Christ. The eclipse was but a warning of what was to come. So intense did the speculations become that the Council of State in England felt duty bound to proclaim that eclipses were natural events and had no other implications. And the governments of France and Sweden feared that important recent events in their realms might be interpreted unfavorably because of the August 1654 eclipse: Louis XIV's coronation had been celebrated on June 7, 1654, and three days later had been the formal date of Queen Christina's abdication from the Swedish throne.

That prophecies and fear of omens should have found so large and receptive an audience is hardly surprising given the long tradition of belief in such phenomena and the upheavals and anxieties of the 1640s and 1650s. What is far more astonishing is the speed with which the obsessions disappeared—a turnabout that is one of the clearest signals that the age we call the Renaissance was over. It is significant, for instance, that in the collections of the Vatican Library books on prophecy and messianism are relatively common in the sixteenth and seventeenth centuries (some ninety titles), but extremely rare thereafter.

A number of scholars have noted this decline, but it has not generally been considered, as is suggested here, central to the fundamental cultural shift of the age. Various explanations have also been offered; among them are the critiques of philosophers, lawyers, clerics, and physicians, who were increasingly insisting on rational argument; the rise of science and its new understanding of nature; and the subsidence of military, political, and social turmoil. It is the latter, in my view, that makes the most sense. As the crisis of mid-century subsided, so too did the power of astrology and prophecy as major influences in western society. It was not so much that the many earnest predictions failed to materialize; it was that the need to believe in them no longer seemed so pressing.

Whatever the reason, the consequences are unmistakable. Despite the resonances of the Year of the Beast, 1666 provoked far less hysteria than the eclipses of 1652 and 1654 (with one exception, to which I will return). In fact, it was in the very year of 1666 that the founding charter of the French Academy of Sciences forbade membership to astrologers. By 1680, an astrologer was complaining that his subject had been banned from Oxford University. And the biblical visionaries, too, were having a dwindling impact. Even one of the most charismatic messiahs of the 1650s, the English prophet James Nayler, who attracted huge followings, calmed down. In his last years, after being severely punished for impolitic predictions in 1657, he sobered up and abandoned his inflammatory rhetoric.

In sum, a formidable cultural and social phenomenon, after centuries of flowering, was equally suddenly in headlong retreat. By the mid-1660s, the notion of invoking "Scripture-prophecy" to help settle a significant political decision, as it had been a mere decade before in that "withdrawing-room in Whitehall," had become unthinkable. Because we now know what lay immediately ahead, we might take one last look at what had been left behind by returning to that discussion, not among hotheads, but in a sober governmental council in December 1655.

The debate over the readmission of the Jews to England is, in this account, a significant marker of the shift in western culture as the Renaissance came to an end. We have here one of the last occasions when biblical verses were thought relevant to issues of governmental policy. Exactly two years before the Whitehall meeting, to the week, the most determined attempt to infuse politics with godliness, the so-called Barebones Parliament, whose membership consisted of 140 designated "saints" from England, Scotland, and Ireland, had come to an ignominious end. Its attempt to establish Mosaic Law as the law of the land was entirely consistent with the need to consult prophecy when considering the readmission of the Jews. But these were the last flourishes of a way of dealing with the world, echoed by the widespread fuss over the eclipses of 1652 and 1654, that lost its centrality in public life thereafter, and became instead a peripheral phenomenon in western society.

In this major shift, Europe's Jews were a remarkably sensitive touchstone. After all, the Hebrew Bible, the basis for so much of the prophecy, was their book. When Henry Finch, back in the 1620s, had promised a new world empire as a precursor to the coming of the Messiah, he had landed in jail because he seemed to be implying the overthrow of the Stuarts. That he was calling for the conversion of the Jews was not held in his favor. Prophecy could seem to offer danger as well as encouragement because, for all the growing claims of skepticism and science, it still had resonance and power. That is why prophets could end up in prison, and also why the argument could be made that the Messiah's coming depended on the ingathering of Jews from all four corners of the earth—that is, from everywhere, including lands from which they had been expelled, such as England.

What is telling about this moment in the passing of an age is that Menasseh ben Israel did not choose to make his case on messianic grounds. And yet that is precisely what might have been expected of him. In the very year that he wrote his famous plea to Cromwell, he published one of the classic millenarian and messianic books of the time, his *Piedra Gloriosa*. This extraordinary work, which explored the meaning of the image of the stone in the Bible—the stone pillow on which Jacob slept when he had his mystical vision of a ladder ascending to heaven, for example, or the stone with which David slew Goliath—offered an unabashed promise of the imminence of the Fifth Monarchy. Indeed, Menasseh even got his friend Rembrandt to illustrate, in addition to the Jacob and David stories, the central text describing the four beasts in the apocalyptic prophecy of Daniel (fig 58). This was the account that had preoccupied Finch and many of the other messianists of the age. The text implies horrors to come, but Rembrandt, down-to-earth as usual, presents the scene as an almost normal occurrence under the watchful eye of heaven:

*Fig. 58 This 1655 engraving by Rembrandt of the four beasts of the Apocalypse takes literally the scene as described in the book of Daniel: God is in his heaven above, and the beasts are invading the earth below.*

And four great beasts came up from the sea, diverse from one another.

The first was like a lion, and had eagle's wings: I beheld till the wings thereof were plucked, and it was lifted up from the earth, and made stand upon the feet as a man, and a man's heart was given to it.

And behold another beast, a second, like to a bear, and it raised up itself on one side, and it had three ribs in the mouth of it between the teeth of it: and they said thus unto it, Arise, devour much flesh.

After this I beheld, and lo another, like a leopard, which had upon the back of it four wings of a fowl; the beast had also four heads; and dominion was given to it.

After this I saw in the night visions, and behold a fourth beast, dreadful and terrible, and strong exceedingly; and it had great iron teeth: it devoured and brake in pieces, and stamped the residue with the feet of it; and it was diverse from all the beasts that were before it; and it had ten horns.

In the end, neither "Scripture-prophecy" nor Menasseh's practical arguments carried the day, and Cromwell decided to shelve his plan for a formal readmission of the Jews. The episode became, instead, a classic instance of English pragmatism and absentmindedness, because the resettlement went ahead anyhow. It is therefore ironic that these two sets of people, the Jews and the English, continued to be moved by apocalyptic visions just a little longer than other Europeans.

When the dread year 1666 arrived, it caused more of a stir in England—possibly because of the great fire that destroyed much of London—than on the Continent. And among the Jews it was the high point of the passion for their most famous "false" Messiah, Shabtai Zvi—a passion that, although attracting considerable attention, did not arouse the prophetic fervor that had disturbed Christian lands in the previous decade. Moreover, England, unlike any other European state, could still feel threatened, as late as the mid-1680s, by a notorious millenarian group, the Fifth Monarchy Men. Amazingly, these heirs of the radicals who in Cromwell's time had been instrumental in the summoning of the Parliament of Saints were still active more than thirty years later.

But that was just about the end of it. Isaac Newton and John Locke were yet to dabble in biblical speculation, but they now did so in private, out of the public eye. And, except for a few diehards, the excitement over Shabtai Zvi vanished as rapidly as it had appeared, expertly defused by the Ottoman government. The days of "Scripture-prophecy" and astrology—both of which had been alive and well during the disruptions and unease associated with the crisis of the mid-seventeenth century—were now over. The millenarians, the messianists, and the astrologers retreated to the fringe position in western societies that they have occupied ever since. Among the arguments for the readmission of the Jews to England, the future lay with economics and pragmatism, not the fading influence of "Scripture-prophecy."

Astrology, cults, divine guidance, and talismans may have remained powerful influences on individuals in the centuries to come, but they no longer played a decisive role in public affairs or in the decisions of governments. An ancient tradition, alive since entrails were examined, sibyls consulted, and prophets obeyed, was to become no more than a private preoccupation. Where once entire societies had been in the thrall of omens and revelatory visions, now it was the ordinary person who might seek certainty in a difficult world through the promise of prediction, whether it be found in the writings of Nostradamus or, more ominously, in warnings about the end of days that, for example, prompted a group's mass suicide when the Hale-Bopp comet approached the earth. There is no question that this unprecedented turning away from a reliance, *in the public sphere,* on the all-pervasive power of the supernatural meant that the new era that was coming into being was unlike any that had ever come before.

∽

That antiwar sentiments could gain respectability in the highest quarters, even as those same leaders of European society could turn their backs on centuries of belief in prophecy, signaled a cultural reorientation of massive proportions. And these transformations merely echoed other, equally decisive, milestones of change: the superiority of antiquity had been undermined; centralized power had been conceded to governments; a new system of international diplomacy had been created; science and reason had swept all before them; and the arts had emerged from an age of striving into an age of decorum. If the Renaissance was over, what would take its place?

*Chapter Seven*

# REVOLUTION AND MODERNITY

*T*he new ambitions that Europeans began to pursue in the years around 1700 have often been summed up as the "Enlightenment project," which encompassed two quests: one for control over nature and the other for a larger degree of social equality. Both of these goals were indeed preoccupations of the period. But they were merely part of a larger enterprise that, though sometimes associated with a notion of modernity, deserves a more descriptive label. When looked at as a totality, the years from around 1700 to around 1900 are best thought of as an era of Revolution.

It is true that most of the features we associate with the eighteenth-century Enlightenment had their origins in the seventeenth century—notably the fascination with science, the consolidation of the European states-system, the ascendancy of the aristocracy, and the expansion of the capitalist economy. Nevertheless, it is appropriate to think of the two centuries that began around 1700 as an era quite distinct from the Renaissance. This was a society that was heading in new directions: It had shaken off the reverence for antiquity; it had raised doubts about the glory of war; it had limited the authority of the supernatural; and it had resolved difficult struggles over centralized political authority and the role of the Church.

The wave of Revolution that had now engulfed Europe had six major components; between them, they shaped the age:

- Political revolution
- Industrial revolution
- Communications revolution
- Social revolution
- Revolution in global relations
- Cultural revolution

A brief elaboration will indicate the nature of these overlapping revolutions.

∞

Political revolution set the tone and distinguished the era from all that had come before; indeed, it permeated every sphere of life. Starting with the War of Independence that created the United States, the movement swept through the West and its colonies. The bureaucratized centralization that had developed during the Renaissance was never seriously challenged, but those who ruled the various states were severely tested. Not only were many new independent regimes established—in Europe itself, with the creation of Italy and Germany, and throughout Central and South America—but governments everywhere had to become more responsive to the wishes of their people. There is no denying that the basic structures of aristocratic power managed to survive even these revolutionary upheavals: An elite of birth remained in control of most institutions until at least 1900. Yet regular concessions had to be made to allow a broadening participation in political affairs, an erosion of privileges such as special tax exemptions, and an acceptance of a larger say for representative bodies. The days of the old aristocracy may have been numbered—the elite now faced serious challenges from reformers and the promoters of new visions of society from Rousseau to Marx—but throughout this Age of Revolution it managed to hang on to its dominant role. Not until late in the period was it clear that traditional political regimes were losing force, and that long-standing loyalties to regions and cities (still a feature of central Europe and Italy, as one can see in Moravia or Bergamo) were, at the same time and for related reasons, being replaced by nationalist feelings.

Essential to the political revolutions sweeping the western world were ambitious social theories, ideologies, and programs that were among the most conspicuous creations of the era. This was the age of "isms." Vast movements, inspired by powerful writers, took hold of the imagination: Liberalism, Socialism, Marxism, and Nationalism were merely the most prominent of the causes that offered blueprints for change to a wider public. But it was not only the writings of philosophers and commentators such as John Stuart Mill, the Comte de Saint-Simon, and Karl Marx that helped change the political landscape. It was also the new forms of propaganda—delivered through newspapers, speeches, literature, and the arts—that helped whip up fervor and mass feelings. In the wake of the French Revolution, with its large-scale mobilizations of manpower and opinion, the nation came to be the focus of individual identity and of grandiose plans for shared advance and glory. The zealous pursuit of nationalist agendas, especially in their external guise, imperialism, was a feature of the age that, when taken to extreme, was ultimately (like the elements of the Renaissance that eventually pushed Europe toward crisis) to help spawn the upheavals that brought the Age of Revolution to an end.

The Industrial Revolution had even more extensive effects. Not only were vast new sources of wealth uncovered but the very organization of economic life was transformed, as theorists from Adam Smith onward demonstrated. New products, from hardened steel to cheap textiles; the factory system, with its marshalling of immensely more extensive resources—human, financial, and material—than ever before; and the accumulation of unprecedented quantities of capital: All helped to create new forms of economic activity, improvements (though uneven) in the standard of living, and rising expectations. Despite regular crises and recoveries, and despite rivalries that encompassed the entire world, the basic story was one of remarkable growth and expanding opportunity. Although many deplored the slowness of political change alongside the economic advance, and the disparities of wealth that were increasingly visible, the era exuded a sense of optimism. Its signal features were a growing recognition of the power of technology, amazement at the miracles it could accomplish, and awareness that new levels of prosperity were being achieved. Progress was the watchword, and many came to assume that capitalism and science might be able to solve most of mankind's problems.

Helping to make all this possible, and itself an outcome of the innovations that drove the economy, was a revolution in communications. First the building of extensive canal networks speeded transportation; then the harnessing of steam power transformed travel by land and sea; and finally, the invention of the telegraph and the telephone made instant connections possible across vast distance. These breakthroughs required huge construction projects, which, in turn, created a new infrastructure of railways, electric and telegraph lines, and roads. By 1900, the isolation of localities that had been a feature of all previous periods had virtually disappeared.

The social consequences of these massive political and economic revolutions were almost endless. The requirements of the factory system stimulated the building of new cities and the rapid growth of old ones. This was the end of the West as an essentially agricultural society. As cities and their economic opportunities became increasingly attractive, moreover, they prompted enormous movements of people. For the first time since the invasions of the early Middle Ages, geographic mobility became the norm. And because the means to make a living were now available to the young (replacing their traditional obligation to work a small family plot until the previous generation died) it became possible for the average age at marriage to drop dramatically, with the result that Europe's population began to soar.

Grappling with the issues raised by these changes, theorists from Thomas Malthus onward laid the foundations for the new academic disciplines of economics and sociology. Ironically, however, it was in this period that one of the perennial connections Malthus uncovered—a decline in wages when population rose—came to an end for the first time in human history. Most impressive about these pioneering studies of economy and society, however, was their reflection of broader changes: a renewed seriousness in universities, which now became centers of research as well as instruction; a proliferation of specialized intellectual pursuits, from political science to musicology; and the development of increasingly elaborate professional structures, whether at newspapers or in scientific laboratories, which in turn created career patterns and forms of organized investigation that were new on the world scene. But there was much more to come.

As cities and disposable income grew, so too did a consumer society. By 1900, London, capital of the richest of these economies, was the largest city the world had ever seen. It had an underground railway, an invisible sewer system, water and electricity distribution networks, plentiful public libraries, and shops that sold goods of a dazzling variety. Every one of these features of city life—and there were many others that would have astonished someone coming from the seventeenth century—transformed the living standards of a large segment of the population. But there was still appalling poverty and irrepressible crime, as the novels of Charles Dickens recorded. One still recoils from the murderous setting in which Bill Sykes operated, or from the first sight of the London slums that the Artful Dodger showed the young Oliver Twist:

> Although Oliver had enough to occupy his attention in keeping sight of his leader, he could not help bestowing a few hasty glances on either side of the way, as he passed along. A dirtier or more wretched place he had never seen. The street was very narrow and muddy, and the air was impregnated with filthy odours. There were a good many small shops; but the only stock in trade appeared to be heaps of children, who, even at that time of night, were crawling in and out at the doors, or screaming from the in-

side. The sole places that seemed to prosper, amid the general blight of the place, were the public-houses; and in them, the lowest orders of Irish were wrangling with might and main. Covered ways and yards, which here and there diverged from the main street, disclosed little knots of houses, where drunken men and women were positively wallowing in filth; and from several of the door-ways, great ill-looking fellows were cautiously emerging, bound, to all appearance, on no very well-disposed or harmless errands.

Nevertheless, even the poor of Dickens's time lived in conditions utterly different from those of the past. Starvation was far less common; the terrible bubonic plagues that had ravaged the Renaissance had died out; and welfare systems capable of remedying the worst deprivations (though often still cruel) were available in many areas. Moreover, a burgeoning campaign to secure basic rights for workers, spearheaded by reformers and the nascent trade union movement, transformed the conditions of labor in the city, limiting daily hours and the employment of children, improving wages, and offering some relief from the weekly grind. For those in the working as well as the middle classes, there was enhanced leisure, and this made possible the development of professional sports, the creation of new facilities such as public parks, and the emergence of hitherto unknown attractions, such as seaside resorts, sunbathing, and mountain climbing. That a larger segment of society was capable of discretionary spending meant that the nineteenth century also saw the birth of the department store. The wider availability of goods confirmed the sense that technology was beginning to ameliorate daily life, and even religious expression reflected the more cheerful emphases of the culture. Thus, for the first time in Christian history, Christmas became more broadly and enthusiastically celebrated than Easter. The transformations, in other words, reached into the very heart of daily life, and they amounted to the most dramatic and far-reaching set of changes in social conditions and relations in so short a period in world history. They were also, without question, one of the central defining features of this Age of Revolution.

At the same time, Europe was becoming embedded in global affairs to an extent that also had never been seen before. The conquests of Alexander the Great and the medieval struggles with the forces of Islam had given the West contacts with civilizations different from its own. And the explorations and overseas settlements of the Renaissance not only had ranged much further but had created more enduring encounters. But none of these earlier ventures could compare with the scale of the imperialist ambitions and the formation of new polities that became so prominent a part of the eighteenth and nineteenth centuries. This was when Europe began, to a significant degree, to reshape the rest of the world and to be reshaped by it. That the relationship was often no less exploitative than it had been in earlier times was clear, but the movements of political independence and the campaigns to abolish slavery suggested that in this arena, too, the world had entered a new era. The gradual establishment of a global economy, marked by ever-more rapid communications, was one of the defining characteristics of the age.

❧

A final mark of the coherence of these centuries was cultural. This was when the lines between elite and popular culture began to blur. As levels of literacy began rapidly to expand, and more than minimal education came to be extended to all levels

*Fig. 59    London's British Museum, holder of a vast collection of art and objects from all periods and places, opened to the public in 1759. It was constantly expanded, and after a major building program in the 1800s it assumed its modern form, seen in this view of 1854, as an enormous classical temple.*

of Europe's population, so too did the carriers of creativity become more widely accessible. Most of the West's great museums and galleries got their start at this time, and from early days they were thrown open to an eager public (fig. 59). Orchestras, opera houses, choral societies, and other producers of music gained huge new audiences in all countries, as did music halls and theaters. There was a level of institutionalization and organization, both of production and of attendance, that was new at all levels, from the most recondite chamber recitals to the most raucous houses of burlesque.

It was a long way from the sophisticated court of a Renaissance prince, where a select few could enjoy the latest compositions or the most advanced productions, to the new world of the fee-charging public performance. Even the high-minded and elaborate enterprise of opera, which in its earliest days was the preserve of the courtier, began to attract an ever wider public from the mid-seventeenth century onward. The new significance that it gradually achieved typified the very different role that the arts assumed in this Age of Revolution.

A perfect example comes from the fraught year of 1789. We usually consider July 14, the day of the storming of the Bastille, as the date that marks the beginning of the French Revolution. Yet it might make just as much sense to push the date back two days, to July 12, 1789, when another Parisian mob—some three thousand strong—invaded a very different public institution, the opera.

That so complex and refined an art as opera—combining as it did instrumental playing, singing, literature, dance, scenic architecture, and costume design—blossomed into one of the central forms of expression of the nineteenth century is indicative of the new situation. Although opera began as a reflection of Baroque ambitions in the seventeenth century, and remained largely an aristocratic interest during the eighteenth, the French Revolution changed all that. However unlikely it may seem to us today, in 1789 the opera house seemed a natural place for a crowd to vent its frustration at the dismissal of a popular minister, Jacques Necker. Because the Parisians of the time regarded opera as elite entertainment, their revenge was to demand that all performances be cancelled. And for the next nine days both the Opéra and the Opéra-Comique remained dark. When they reopened, moreover, their themes began to change radically. Instead of libretti that celebrated beloved rulers, selfless aristocrats, and benevolent clergy, there began to appear stories of heroic commoners, rescues from evil officials (Beethoven's *Fidelio* is a famous example), and struggles against the severity of Church authorities. It was precisely because opera had enjoyed such standing and significance that the French insurgents felt so strongly the need to block its conservative message and then put on performances that advanced their revolutionary program.

The result was a broad recognition, lasting throughout the nineteenth century, that opera could be a powerful political force. After all, from its earliest days its patrons had regarded it as an effective way to endorse the traditional social hierarchy and support the authority of such princely and royal dynasties as the Gonzagas in Mantua, the Stuarts in England, and the Bourbons in France. Now, however, as it became a more popular form—and ordinary people were heard humming the famous chorus "Va Pensiero" only days after the premiere of the opera in which it was first sung, Giuseppe Verdi's *Nabucco*—it began to exert its power in new directions. Verdi's is the most famous example of a composer who aroused the wrath of the authorities over operas that they (and the audiences) regarded as subversive. But he was by no means the first. Already in 1813, long before Italian unification was seriously contemplated, Gioacchino Rossini had inserted into a comic opera (of all places) a remarkable rondo, "Pensa alla Patria," about love of country. The heroine of *The Italian Girl in Algiers* urges on the pusillanimous men she encounters with the words:

*If Country, Duty, Honor,*
*Speak to your heart, then learn*
*From the others to be an Italian;*

*And in the events*
*Of fickle destiny, let a woman*
*Teach you to be strong.*
*Think of your country, and fearless*
*Carry out your duty:*
*See that for all of Italy*
*Examples are born anew*
*Of valor and daring.*

Yet it was above all in Verdi—in the conspiracies, assassinations, and calls to liberty of his early works, notably *I Lombardi, Ernani,* and *Attila*—that people read the comments on Italy's subjection to the Austrians that sparked public demonstrations. To this day, the blood courses more quickly as one listens to the stirring male duets made famous by nineteenth-century Italian operas—from "Suoni la tromba" in Bellini's *Puritani* to "Dio che nell'alma infondere" in Verdi's *Don Carlo*—overflowing with patriotism, the promise of courage, and a fight to the death for freedom. Fearing the emotion Verdi could arouse, the authorities forced the composer to shift the setting of *Un Ballo in Maschera* from Stockholm, where a king had in fact been murdered half a century earlier, to seventeenth-century Boston. Even *Rigoletto,* about an amoral prince, got him into trouble. And soon Verdi's name became an acronym for the cry of the revolutionaries who wanted the king of Piedmont to become king of Italy: Vittorio Emmanuele Re D'Italia! The cry "Viva la Liberta!" that was uttered in Mozart's *Don Giovanni* a few decades earlier had been transformed into "Viva Verdi!"

All this was a long way from the criticism of aristocratic privilege in the celebrated adaptations by Mozart and Rossini of two comic French masterpieces, *The Marriage of Figaro* and

*The Barber of Seville,* or the more general social commentary in *Don Giovanni.* From Rossini's *William Tell* to Smetana's *Brandenburgers in Bohemia,* the persistence of the summons to patriotic fervor or simply to freedom turned opera into a major form of political expression.

And in one remarkable instance, it led directly to revolution. On August 25, 1830, there was a performance in Brussels of *La Muette de Portici,* the one serious work among the usually comic operas of Daniel Auber. Based on the events of a popular uprising in Naples in 1647 led by a fisherman, Masaniello (a true episode from the seventeenth-century "crisis"), *La Muette* has not remained a staple of the repertory. But in 1830 its themes were so incendiary that, as the audience left the opera house, it began to riot, demanding freedom from Dutch rule. The unrest gathered strength during the days that followed and eventually grew into a full-scale uprising that won the Belgians, within a few months, an independent state and their own constitution.

The newfound role of opera was the most dramatic instance of the reorganization of cultural expression and the crossing of traditional cultural lines that marked this age, but it was not alone. The invention of the public concert, the professionalization of the orchestra, the regularization of sales of art, and the proliferation of publishers all meant that the classic reliance of artists, composers, musicians, and writers on wealthy patrons was coming to an end. The "democratization" of opera was thus merely one part of a transformation that set the Age of Revolution apart from all its predecessors.

But this age, too, came to an end. Immense pressures were mounting as demands rose for an end to aristocratic privilege, for extensions of the franchise, and for wider political participation;

as the effects of economic change took hold; as shifts in global relations and imperialist ambitions created a new international landscape; as movements gathered strength for the emancipation of women (it is hard now to recover the shock caused by Henrik Ibsen's 1879 *A Doll's House*) and religious minorities; and as waves of cultural innovation arose, from Friedrich Nietzsche's assaults on traditional morality and Christianity to the Impressionists' questioning of the fundamentals of artistic endeavor. These intensifying onslaughts on traditional structures and assumptions finally caused upheavals of an intensity that surpassed all the crises that had come before. By comparison, the events of the Thirty Years' War, the mid-seventeenth century, and the decades of revolutionary turmoil around 1800 seemed minor as two World Wars, vast depressions, and an overturning of centuries of cultural assumptions swept through what was now a global civilization.

⚘

It is a long way from the time of Charlemagne, where we began, to the twentieth century. Yet the establishment and eventual dissolution of coherences in culture and society have been a constant theme. Just as the distinct eras of the Middle Ages, the Renaissance, and the Age of Revolution came together and then came apart, so too has there been a shift toward new structures and hints of gradual coalescence in the era that has followed— which, for the time being, we might as well call "Modernity," though it may come to be seen as the First Global Age. Some regard the Age of Revolution as Modernity and distinguish the twentieth century as postmodern, but such semantic jugglings are ephemeral and self-defeating. What is unequivocal is that in the decades around 1900, the set of coherences we associate with the Age of Revolution began to dissolve. Although it is much too early to offer predictions about where subsequent developments are heading, or what the new set of unities will be, it is not difficult to describe, in outline, the break with the past that took place during those years around 1900.

The most obvious departure was in esthetics. All areas of artistic creativity determinedly turned their backs on the traditions of the preceding eras. And it is significant that those who were at the forefront of change, from Beaudelaire to Schönberg, themselves described their campaign as a "modern movement," the fashioning of a "modern" outlook. It is no surprise that Charlie Chaplin named his remarkable 1936 film about a world that was changing all its bearings *Modern Times*. In these years music rejected tonality, painting rejected representation (fig. 60), poetry rejected rhyme and meter, prose rejected narrative, and architecture rejected familiar forms and structures. As if to draw a line, the Museum of Modern Art in New York refused to allow work created before the 1880s to enter its collection. Every standard of beauty that the Renaissance had stood for, despite having survived the succeeding age, was now called into question. The qualities of accident and chance, of deliberate obfuscation, of dissonance and disharmony, came to the fore. All promises of confident assurance were found empty. Even within science, once the model for orderliness and the power of thought, the reliance on predictable structures gave way to theories of randomness and doubt. The new emphasis on relativity and uncertainty in the physical world, proposed by Albert Einstein, Werner Heisenberg, and their colleagues, was echoed in ideas about human nature as Sigmund Freud and others took a critical look at long-standing claims about the possibility of rational thought.

*Fig. 60    Picasso's* Still Life with Violin *of 1912 is a perfect example of the revolution in art wrought by the cubist movement in the early twentieth century. It rejects the representational aims that had dominated painting since the early Renaissance and instead seeks the essence of a form by looking at its elements from different angles simultaneously. Traditional esthetics had become unrecognizable, and thereafter artistic experimentation headed in a multitude of new directions.*

In just a brief period around 1900, therefore, Europe witnessed a breathtaking and deliberate assault on the inheritance from the past. It was a shift in direction as definitive as the one we saw unfold in the mid-seventeenth century, and even more rapid. Virginia Woolf put it bluntly: "In or about December, 1910, human character changed." D. H. Lawrence may have given it a few more years—"It was in 1915 the old world ended"—but the instincts of these sensitive observers, even if semijocular in this context, are not to be dismissed. That James Joyce's *Ulysses,* T. S. Eliot's *Waste Land,* and Franz Kafka's *Trial* and *Castle* were all to be published between 1922 and 1926 is an indication that Woolf and Lawrence were prescient indeed. Moreover, the sense of lost moorings and crisis that ensued was reinforced, as it had been in the sixteenth century, by upheavals in other areas of life.

The steady surrender by the traditional elite of its hold on social and political power was evidenced by the unheard-of extension of the franchise to women throughout the West. But that was not enough of a change for those, on the left as well as on the right, who were demanding a radical overhaul of society. If fascism was a last desperate attempt to restore a firm, unshakable order in a crumbling world, socialism and communism sought to advance the claims of ordinary people to new heights. The terrible clashes that grew out of these diametrically opposed positions created horrors, in the years between 1914 and 1945—exacerbated by a worldwide depression that the new economic institutions were supposed to have prevented—that left the disasters of earlier centuries looking tame by comparison. There was no escaping the conclusion that the mayhem unleashed in 1914, followed by increasingly devastating shocks as the full ghastliness of human behavior in the

1930s and 1940s came to light, made it inconceivable that old outlooks could ever be restored. Nor could the political boundaries that had held sway for centuries survive the snowballing demand for ethnic and national self-determination that followed Woodrow Wilson's formulation of the principle in his "Fourteen Points" speech in 1918.

At the same time, the wonders of technology and economic advance of the previous age seemed to turn sour. Man's "conquest" of the natural world was now seen as threatening to destroy it; the unimaginable levels of speed that were achieved in communications and travel only intensified the dangers; and the new levels of economic capacity and global interdependence, instead of promoting social progress and prosperity, seemed only to exacerbate the exploitation of the weak and widen the disparities of wealth throughout the world. The loudly proclaimed quest for equality of gender, race, and economic opportunity for all often seemed no more than rhetoric. Balancing the spread of education, in the view of many critics, were the numbing effects of much of popular culture. Parts of Asia may have enjoyed a rapidly rising standard of living, but much of Africa suffered disaster. For all the advances in food production and ease of communication, neither poverty nor repressive regimes were losing ground. It was no wonder, therefore, that in the second half of the twentieth century, theorists of culture and ideas challenged such notions as "meaning" or "purpose" in human endeavors, and dismissed the possibility of finding "truth" or "reality" in any area of history or creative work. Even the flowering of two new art forms made possible by technology, photography and film—both of which were able to create ever more startling effects through yet another invention devoted to high speed, manipulation, and "virtual reality," the computer—seemed merely to underline how specious appearances could be, how untrustworthy our senses, how "constructed" our notions of reality.

At the same time, it had become clear by the late twentieth century that it no longer made sense to think of the West as the distinctive civilization it had been since at least the age of Charlemagne. Large movements of people now encompassed the entire planet. Although English was rapidly becoming the standard language for worldwide communication (replacing the French, the *lingua franca*, that had dominated diplomacy during the Age of Revolution), it was telling that, on the streets of central London in the 1990s, foreign tongues were more common than English. It no longer made sense for mammoth corporations to be merely international in scope; their production and their markets had to be global. That radical antiglobalization and environmental movements now sought to counter what they saw as the exploitation and pollution inflicted by these corporations (and by the governments that encouraged them) was a sure sign that local and regional autonomies had dissolved. Increasingly, musical and theatrical performances, translations of works of literature, and purchases of works of art recognized no cultural boundaries. The erosion of frontiers within the European community was but one indication of this larger process as political, economic, and intellectual entities, once distinct, began to blur at the edges.

With the questions about the old certainties of the Age of Revolution intensifying, and with the various forms of globalization accelerating the decline of national identities, reaction was inevitable. In the same way as the rationalism of the Enlightenment prompted the Romantics to call for a return to the emotions, so the growing skepticism, internationalism, and materialism of the decades after World War II have been met by a resurgence of moral and religious passion and demands for a reassertion of "traditional" values and local interests. The contest between these forces, often reduced to such simple dichotomies as The Market vs. The Welfare State or Islam vs. The West or even The Culture Wars, may cause ever-widening cleavages and ever fiercer battles. If the past is any guide, however, it will eventually become clear how the world wishes to move forward, and the coherences of the age will take shape anew.

If all this seems reminiscent of the mushrooming crisis of the seventeenth century, it may be that historians looking back will come to see what we have called Modernity as merely the last, turbulent phase of the Age of Revolution. Either way, it is much too early to reach conclusions about the outcome of the turbulence. If that seems too gloomy a prospect, though, it is worth recalling the clarity of the resolution of that previous crisis: the fundamental change that overtook the West in the decades leading up to 1700. I have argued that periodization is the essential armature on which all of history rests, and that the great transitions that began and ended the Renaissance remain the fundamental landmarks in the story of Europe since the fall of the Roman Empire. But that argument also has relevance for those who lament the need to struggle through a time when yet another such painful transition is under way; indeed, it could be useful to face that challenge through the lens of historical understanding. In the words of the Book of Proverbs, knowledge increases strength, and it may well be that an awareness of the major presiding assumptions of our past, and of the movements for change that undermined them and brought us to where we are, will help to dispel the gloom. As we trace these stabilities and progressions across the centuries, we should be able to take heart, in particular, from the resilience and optimism that emerged from a period that bears such close resemblance to our own, the last days of the Renaissance.

# Suggestions for Further Reading

Providing a full scholarly apparatus for this book, which is basically an extended essay, would have meant doubling its length, and doing so primarily as a service for historians already familiar with the literature of the field. That seemed unnecessary. For the general reader who wishes to explore this subject matter further, however, it may be useful to indicate some of the major landmarks in the literature.*

The two monuments that defined the Renaissance for modern scholarship were Jacob Burckhardt, *The Civilization of the Renaissance in Italy* (1860) and Johan Huizinga, *The Waning of the Middle Ages* (1919). The many interpretations up to 1948 were summarized by Wallace Ferguson, *The Renaissance in Historical Thought* (1948). Since then, overviews have appeared regularly, but the most comprehensive single volume, elegantly written, is John Hale, *The Civilization of Europe in the Renaissance* (1993).

As a reference work and also an opportunity to encounter unexpected delights, Gordon Campbell's *The Oxford Dictionary of the Renaissance* (2003) is both up-to-date and unmatched.

The weakening hold of Renaissance concerns in the seventeenth century has been less intensively studied, but three books explored the cultural shift of the age at some length: Paul Hazard, *The Crisis of the European Conscience* (1935); William Bouwsma, *The Waning of the Renaissance* (2000); and Jonathan Israel, *Radical Enlightenment* (2001).

Beyond these general works, there are particular topics from the period that have inspired splendid and readable books. To name a dozen favorites from the last half century or so, covering a broad range of Renaissance themes, I would recommend, in order of publication: Herbert Butterfield, *The Origins of Modern Science* (1949); Erwin Panofsky, *Meaning in the Visual Arts* (1955); Garrett Mattingly, *The Armada* (1959); Hugh Trevor-Roper, *Religion the Reformation and Social Change* (1967); Fernand Braudel, *Civilization and Capitalism* (1967); John Elliott, *The Old World and the New 1492–1650* (1970); Keith Thomas, *Religion and the Decline of Magic* (1971); Roy Strong, *Splendor at Court* (1973); Robert Evans, *Rudolf II and his World* (1973); Carlo Ginzburg, *The Cheese and the Worms* (1976); Lawrence Stone, *The Family, Sex and Marriage in England 1500–1800* (1977); and Elizabeth & Thomas Cohen, *Daily Life in Renaissance Italy* (2001).

---

⋆ Dates are of first publication, even if the English version (as cited) appeared later.

# Index